# SHORNE

## The History of a Kentish Village

# SHORNE

## THE HISTORY OF A KENTISH VILLAGE

A.F. ALLEN

MERESBOROUGH BOOKS
1987

Published by Meresborough Books, 17 Station Road, Rainham, Kent. ME8 7RS.

Meresborough Books is a specialist publisher of books about Kent. A list of titles available at the time of going to press is printed at the back of this book.

© Copyright 1987 A.F. Allen
ISBN 0948193204

Printed by Whitstable Litho Ltd, Whitstable, Kent.

## CONTENTS

| | | |
|---|---|---:|
| Chapter 1 | Introduction, Prehistory, Roman and Anglo Saxon Shorne | 7 |
| Chapter 2 | The Early Church and Manor | 17 |
| Chapter 3 | Other Manors and a Medieval Mystery | 23 |
| Chapter 4 | The Later Medieval Church, Manor and People | 29 |
| Chapter 5 | Medieval Epilogue | 35 |
| Chapter 6 | The Development of the Parish | 41 |
| Chapter 7 | Charity and the Poor | 45 |
| Chapter 8 | The Civil War and Shorne | 51 |
| Chapter 9 | Restoration and Stability | 61 |
| Chapter 10 | The Dover Road, Inns and Tanneries | 67 |
| Chapter 11 | The Landed Gentry and their Estates | 73 |
| Chapter 12 | The Poor and the Overseers | 81 |
| Chapter 13 | An Eighteenth Century Vicar | 87 |
| Chapter 14 | The Preservation of Charity | 95 |
| Chapter 15 | The Poor House | 101 |
| Chapter 16 | War and Peace | 105 |
| Chapter 17 | The Return of the Lords of Cobham Hall | 111 |
| Chapter 18 | The Last Days of the Manor | 117 |
| Chapter 19 | The Church and School | 121 |
| Chapter 20 | Victorian Shorne | 127 |
| Chapter 21 | The Later Victorian Church | 133 |
| Chapter 22 | The Turn of the Century | 139 |
| Chapter 23 | The Changing Village | 145 |
| Index | | 155 |

## Chapter 1
## INTRODUCTION, PREHISTORY, ROMAN AND ANGLO SAXON SHORNE

**Introduction**

Halfway between the Thameside town of Gravesend and the City of Rochester upon Medway, the rural parish of Shorne, with its three thousand or so acres, stretches from the international highway of the river Thames to the A2 motorway which links Dover with London along the route once used by the Romans. Less than thirty miles from the heart of London and but two or three miles from the outskirts of two large towns, the parish is rapidly losing its ancient rural character. This history is an attempt to record its story before all is lost in urban expansion.

Although some three to four hundred houses have been built in and around the parish during the past thirty or forty years, much of the older village yet survives. Picturesque and hilly roads, with their sudden distant views of the Thames and the Essex Hills beyond, the high Ridgeway from which both Thames and Medway can be glimpsed, the wooded hills and the arable pattern of the lower fields sloping towards the Thameside marshes form the background of this history.

The southern boundary of the parish dividing Shorne from the adjoining parish of Cobham, extending for some two miles from Park Pale in the east to Clay Lane Woods in the west, is the A2 main road. The eastern boundary between Shorne and the parish of Higham follows a generally northerly direction with many angles and turns, suggesting long forgotten topographical features, until it reaches the Thames, a distance of some three miles as the crow flies. The northwestern boundary between Shorne and the neighbouring parish of Chalk follows a north easterly direction along banks and hedges (except where already obliterated by the houses of the Gravesend Riverview estate), until it also reaches the river bank. The distance between the two bounds on the river frontage is a bare half mile.

Geologically the southern half of the parish consists of Blackheath and Woolwich beds of sand and gravel overlaid in part by a thick layer of London Clay, the whole forming hills rising some three hundred and fifty feet above the river level. A tongue of these beds forms the Ridgeway with its hamlet of Shorne Ridgeway which links the higher ground with Gads Hill and the lower hills of the Hundred of Hoo, whilst another spur of gravelly soil to the west of the Ridgeway ends in two prominent hills, Shorne Hill and Barrow Hill. On Shorne Hill the village windmill once stood, and against the eastern flank of Shorne Hill, in the dip between the two hills, is the main hamlet of the village called the Street, with the church and the village shops. Against the western flank of Shorne Hill is the small hamlet of Shorne Ifield. All this hill country is heavily wooded, Randall, Crabbles, Brewers, Shorne, and Court woods covering several hundred acres.

The wide arable fields to the north of the hills mark where the underlying chalk of the whole district comes to the surface, and a line of small chalk pits across this part of the parish tells of the use to which this substrata has been put during the centuries for agriculture, limeburning and building material. In this part of the parish are two more hamlets, Thong, well to the west of the main part of the parish, and Lower Shorne, or Marshside as it was once called, where the chalk dips under the alluvial clays and gravels of the Thameside marshes, which provide a milewide area of marsh grazing, once an important part of the agricultural economy of the village.

The clays and gravels of the high ground have many springs which form small streams. Although these streams are now intercepted before they reach the Thames, they once formed an essential part of the scene. They collected into two main courses. One, the eastern collection, no doubt formed the basis of the original settlement at Shorne Street. It still flows to the east of the churchyard, but less than half a mile further on after being piped for two or three hundred yards, it is intercepted by a swallow hole in a chalk pit in Swillers Lane. In earlier times it flowed on through the fields until it reached the Thames, and it seems probable that the wandering ditch which still marks the parish boundary between Shorne and Higham in the marsh land area is the line of the original stream. The other system, deriving its water from two main sources in the western woods, was probably once the basis of the two hamlets of Thong and Shorne Ifield. Although now intercepted by lakes formed by the landscaping of the Cobham Hall estates by a former Earl of Darnley, and by a swallow hole in Shorne Ifield, this stream, like its eastern fellow, once flowed across the lower ground to the Thames, and where it crossed the marshes it formed the parish boundary between Shorne and Chalk. It may be mentioned that even in the most drought stricken times these two streams maintain a flow of water. At their probable point of junction with the Thames were small inlets which, until the river was embanked, formed creeks which the small craft of those early days could use.

**Prehistory**

The first traces of man in the district are associated with the fundamentals of geology. On the heath lands of Randall Heath in the hills south of Shorne Ifield, and in the gardens of Hill House on the edge of the Ridgeway, each with its small stream running in the valley near the site, a scatter of mesolithic flint flakes have been found, suggesting that these two high places on gravelly heathland soil with their nearby streams were once favoured camping grounds of the mesolithic hunter. Indeed, on the barren brackens of Randall Heath one can imagine that the scene has changed little since the hunters camped there perhaps five thousand years ago.

A somewhat later trace of prehistoric man can still be seen in a series of Bronze Age barrows which, as circular field marks, show and fade with the crops and climate on the wide fields of Thong and Chalk on either side of the valley in which the westernmost of Shorne's streams once ran. At least five rings have been observed as crop marks in this area and two have been examined by excavation.[1] The first by Mr George Payne in about 1908 and the other by the writer in 1970. Mr Payne found burials and had no hesitation in treating his finds as Bronze Age. The second dig, though revealing ditches similar to the earlier excavation, produced little further evidence beyond the fact that it had been a mound, levelled (from such evidence as the stem of a clay pipe supplies) in the late eighteenth or early nineteenth century. An indication of the relatively recent date of the levelling of the site is the name 'Chalky Nob' which still attaches to the field.

**The Roman Scene**

Shorne still bears a mark of the Roman occupation in the southern boundary of the parish, which follows the line of the Roman highway from Dover to London. In Cobham Park, a few hundred yards south of the highway at the point where Shorne Ridgeway forms a junction with it, a small Roman villa stood, probably erected on the site of an earlier Iron Age Settlement during the first century of the occupation.

The principal Roman remains in the parish, however, have been found in the area of the riverside marshes and the river bank itself, introducing some interesting speculations about the geography of the area and the activities of the Romano-Briton in the district at that time.

These finds form part of the series of Roman remains which have come to light over the past century along the whole of what are now the marshside boundaries of the Thames from Chalk in the west to the Isle of Grain in the Hundred of Hoo. In Shorne, in the complex area which today comprises the decaying Thames and Medway Canal, the railway and the factory complex known locally as the Uralite works, many Roman finds have been reported. Indeed, were the site not so submerged under modern industry and railway sidings it might well repay investigation by modern archaeological methods. The old reports are tantalising. Mr Crafter, a Victorian archaeologist, reports that, whilst deepening the canal in 1810 opposite Kings Farm (which at that time stood between the Canal and the present Queens Farm), quantities of pottery were found in a field called Potters Field. In 1847 he reports that, whilst cutting the line of the railway to the south of the canal, funeral urns and other Roman material were uncovered. He further observes that near Stonewick Bridge, in a field between the canal and the railway called Stonewick Field, Roman roof tiles, mortar and stones were found. This field is the approximate site of the present Uralite works and when the works were constructed at the beginning of the twentieth century further Roman material was found and a few pots were preserved by the Company. A gravel pit between the canal and the railway also produced further finds of Roman pottery and what appear to have been kilns according to the reports of both Roach Smith and George Payne, two later Kentish archaeologists, whilst another gravel pit nearby to the south of the railway is reported as having produced Roman pottery.

All these finds are about a mile from the banks of the Thames, and from Stonewick Bridge a landway still leads to Higham Causeway which stretches, lonely and bare, to the river bank. In Roman times, and indeed until the eighteenth century, this causeway was the eastern bank of an inlet from the river, which was in use until late medieval times as the Kentish side of a ferry which crossed the river to Essex at this point. The causeway still projects beyond the present river wall well into the rapidly eroding saltings beyond the wall and obviously long preceded the construction of the present river wall. As the saltings wash away they yield up quantities of Roman pottery indicating a considerable Roman settlement on the river bank at this point, and during the last seven or eight years several Roman burials of the first or second centuries have been found slowly washing out of the river mud, well below the present high water mark. Clearly at the beginning of the Christian era, the river at this point was narrower and less tidal than it is today, with its banks well above the tide levels, consisting of meadows in which Roman burials could be sited. Where the swift tides of the Thames now flow was a sizeable Roman community, no doubt based on the inlet from the river, a useful harbour for local fishing boats and the ferry.

The causeway not only connected the settlement around Stonewick Bridge with the riverside settlement, but also formed the link between the Kentish hinterland and a ferry across the Thames to the Essex shore and East Anglia. There is some evidence that this ferry was of considerable antiquity even in Roman times. An ancient footpath system can still be followed from the riverside at this point across Shorne Ridgeway, Cobham Park and the Cuxton Valley to the Halling hills where it joins the ancient prehistoric 'Pilgrims Way' across the south of England at the point where that way crosses the Medway.

In Roman times Shorne Ridgeway formed a link between the Roman road from Dover to London and the Ferry, whilst another trackway can be traced from Shorne Ridgeway along the spur of hills which ends in Shorne Hill, down the deeply sunken Crown Lane and across the fields of Green Farm to Stonewick Bridge. Beside the Ridgeway route Roman burials have been found, and beside Crown Lane (according to an old villager once called Caesars Lane) Roman coins have been reported. On the northern side of the river opposite the site of the Roman settlement on the Kentish shore on the slightly higher ground of East Tilbury, roads still lead northward with Roman directness towards Chelmsford, once a Roman town.

The importance of the ferry in the first century of Roman occupation is clear when it is remembered that the first Roman capital in Britain was at Colchester. To a Roman landing at Dover the crossing at Higham would provide a decidedly shorter journey to that capital than the river crossing at London. This tilts the argument which has gone on in antiquarian circles for many years, from Hasted, the eighteenth century Kentish historian, to the present day, about the probable Thames crossing place of the retreating Britons and the advancing Roman army during the Claudian invasion.[2]

The Roman historian Dio Cassius records that after a hard battle at the crossing of the Medway at Rochester, the British forces retreated, crossing the Thames at some undefined spot followed by Plautius and his troops. May a local historian sum up all that can be detected locally about the possibility of that crossing being at Higham rather than in the London area.

The Roman historian says that the Rochester battle was finally won by a turning movement by troops under Vespasian, who crossed the Medway probably to the south of the main crossing at Rochester. The topography of the western bank of the Medway suggests that this attack was on the line of the Cuxton Valley turning northward in an attempt to cut off the Britons from their probable line of retreat towards London. One may for a moment speculate whether the name Battle Street in Cobham is some ancient folk memory of the battle, and the somewhat ill-recorded find of a mass grave with armour in the fields of Thong about half a mile south of Battle Street[3] may have nothing to do with this Roman battle, but Vespasian was an energetic and capable commander who would seek to encircle the defeated Britons to prevent them from retreating westward.

Faced with a threat to their flank and rear, the crossing of the Thames at Higham was the obvious course, rather than a long retreat (a days march) to crossings in the London area, particularly as Colchester was the British capital. There is evidence to support the suggestion that the Romans themselves, after reorganisation, crossed the river at this point. On the high ground on which Chalk church stands, a couple of hundred yards west of the Shorne parish boundary, recent excavation for a gas main revealed a series of substantial ditches containing Roman material. The ditches could not be properly examined because of the speed of the trenching operation of the Gas Board, but sufficient of the ditch was revealed to show that it was a military type trench suggesting a Roman marching camp. The site overlooks the whole of the river bank and the ferry crossing, suggesting that one Roman unit at least was posted on this commanding position to cover the Roman forces against any attack from the London direction whilst they organised their crossing of the river at Higham.

Apart from the finds at Stonewick Field two patches of Roman occupation have been dug through on the Marsh itself. One just within the present river wall, and the other further inland a couple of hundred yards or so from the Canal Bank. Neither of these finds could be investigated because the substrata of the marshes is semi-liquid clay, the holes filling with water in a matter of hours, but Roman pottery in fair quantity was observed.

The neighbouring parish of Chalk has not only a series of kilns and much kiln waste in a gravel pit adjoining the Shorne boundary, but also a quite notable villa complex which consists of two buildings within a hundred yards of each other. The western of the two was a villa building with a basement, probably dating from the first century and destroyed by fire at the end of the third century. No attempt seems to have been made to rebuild the place after the fire, although the building showed signs of having been quite extensively rebuilt in earlier times. In the basement under the fire debris were signs that barley and apples were stored there, whilst in one corner were found bone pins in all stages of manufacture. The hollow formed by the collapsed building was used as a dump by the inhabitants of the settlement until at least the end of the fourth century.

The other building to the east was a substantial bathhouse structure with a large hypocaust. It has been extensively robbed of all its usable building material, probably in medieval times (Chalk church half a mile away has much reused Roman material in its walls) and so its story is obscure. It seems to have been erected at about the same time as the nearby basement house (though no direct connection between the two could be detected) and altered from time to time during the period of occupation. The remains include concrete foundations some three feet thick which suggest it was a substantial building, but the absence of any indications of the usual luxury of the bath houses of Roman villas suggests perhaps some industrial use.

All these finds lie in a line roughly where the ground rises above the marsh levels, and the fields of Shorne to the south of this line have so far revealed no traces of Roman occupation. They have one common factor — a degeneration between the early period and the final end of the settlements. The failure to rebuild the burnt out basement house at the end of the third century, even though the area continued to be occupied for another hundred years, was preceded by the apparent cessation of the potteries, none of which can be confidently dated after the end of the second century. The picture is repeated in a find made as long ago as 1883 in Cobham Park, only a short distance from the then undiscovered Roman villa there. A pot containing over 800 Roman coins covering the period between 306 and 361 was found which was then thought to be the hoard of some traveller on the highway, but now seems likely to represent the savings of the last inhabitant of the villa who buried his fortune before hiding from some invader, never to return, leaving his home to decay.

The most evocative find of this period is the half dozen or so inhumations found near the second century potteries in Lower Chalk near the Shorne boundary. All the associated grave goods were late fourth century, some of it so worn as to suggest long use before being buried, save one article from an earlier, perhaps more prosperous time — a Samian dish of the Antonine period, worn but intact, though probably over a hundred years old when placed in the grave. It must have been a family heirloom, and was a last offering to whatever gods there were, as a propitiation in those disturbed times. The burials were, however, all in wooden coffins, lying roughly north to south, the feet, in the hobnailed boots of the coloni of those days, to the south.

The decline, apart from the general decline in the Roman civilisation, can be attributed to two factors. The original importance of the ferry must have declined when the centre of Roman rule became established in London, and there is some indication of a change in river levels during the Roman occupation. The evidence is slight, but points to a 'surge' such as was experienced in 1953 rather than a general lowering of land levels. The Roman remains found within the present river wall by the massive excavation of clay to raise the wall after the 1953 tide seem to have been in two layers divided by a thin line of turf decayed into peat. This suggests the site was abandoned because of flooding, but a return was made after a period when it was found the flooding was not repeated.

**The Anglo-Saxon Period**

The earliest traces of Anglo Saxon occupation in the Shorne district are, somewhat surprisingly, in the archaeologically rich area around Stonewick Bridge and the Uralite works. George Payne, in his report of Roman finds referred to earlier, says that 'contiguous to the above' Anglo Saxon interments were found. They seem to have been in the gravel diggings, and he says were cut through 'in the most reckless way' with the result that only a few articles were recovered, though they included a small bronze mounted bucket now in Rochester museum. Faint echoes of this particular discovery were still to be heard in the village until recently, old villagers recalling that the gravel diggers would call at the local public houses with finds to sell to anyone with the price of a drink.

Apart from these finds the Anglo Saxon period of our history is restricted to one or two written records and the appearance of localities which can still be identified, which indicate that during this period the outlines of the village community we now know were being formed.

The name Shorne is based on the Saxon word 'Scora'. 'The Oxford Dictionary of Place Names' suggests the word means a steep slope.[4] The site of the village against the steep slopes of Shorne Hill confirm the probability of this derivation. By the end of the Saxon period Shorne was a sufficiently established place to find itself amongst the vills comprising the Hundred of Shamwell, Shamel, or Escammels, part of the Lathe of Aylesford. According to Hasted the hundred contained twelve villages: Halling, Cuxton, Cobham, Shorne, Chalk, Denton, Merston, Higham, Cliffe, Cooling, Frindsbury and Strood. All these villages, except Merston, are still villages or parts of towns known by their ancient names and we may assume that they were vills of sufficient size and population to be treated as part of the administrative system when the hundreds were developed.

Something of the changes which were taking place during these centuries can however be traced in the earliest written record affecting the district. In 774 King Offa gave certain lands in Higham to Rochester Cathedral and details of the grant are preserved amongst the Rochester Cathedral archives. The bounds of the grant to the east are not relevant to this history, but the descriptions of the western boundary throws light on the district with which this history is concerned. The bounds here, we are told, were 'Mersctune', 'Bulenham' and 'Merscfleot'.[5]

There can be little doubt that 'Merscfleot' is the creek from the Thames which in Roman times had been the landing place of the cross Thames ferry to East Anglia. The other two places can be identified from later records, though only their names survive today. 'Bulenham' must have been approximately in the area of the Roman settlement near Stonewick Bridge. Its general location is suggested by the curious survival of place names in the locality. Two fields to the south of Stonewick Field were called Hither and Further Bull Fields. The Shorne marshes have, from medieval times at least, had an area near the site of the creek known first as Boleham Meadow, later as Boleham Marsh, and then later again as Boleham Salts. Nearby in Higham is Bull Lane. It does not seem hard to imagine that one of the raiding Anglo Saxon ships finding the creek a convenient harbour settled in the old Roman village so conveniently at the head of the creek under the chieftainship of one 'Bull' or under the fighting totem of the 'bull' from which their settlement was to derive its name.

Before the end of the Saxon period this ancient locality had changed its name to that of Bickley. There is a small hill known as Bickley Hill, near Stonewick Bridge to the north of the canal, and nearby two lonely cottages known as Bickley Cottages once stood. In Domesday Book there was a small manor of Bichelie of half a ploughland, but with a mill – no doubt a watermill based on the stream from the uplands of Shorne which then flowed nearby. In later years this small manor came into the hands of the wealthy de Cobham family and for convenience, no doubt, was amalgamated with the Manor of Chalk on the other side of the Shorne lands. This curious administrative arrangement continued when parishes became administrative entities and, until the readjustment of boundaries in the nineteenth century, this part of the marshes and lowlands of Shorne and Higham was known as 'Chalk Extra', comprising about 130 acres around Stonewick Bridge including Hither and Further Bull Fields. In this strange survival we may detect the outline of the Domesday manor and perhaps less clearly the Anglo Saxon 'Bulanham'.

'Mersctune' introduces an interesting example within our present parish boundaries of a lost Saxon and Medieval village known as 'Merston'. Unlike Bulanham or Bickley, which was soon to fade from the records as a hamlet leaving only its name, 'Mersctune' was to survive until the fourteenth century and to be one of the vills of the Saxon Hundred. It will come into this history again, but today its remains (including the foundations of a small Norman church) now lie under the fields of Green Farm and the principal trace now showing in crop marks is that of a rectangular ditch, the outline enclosing some four acres of land showing from time to time where once was a stockaded Saxon village.

These three Anglo Saxon localities have now all become but names and another record from the end of the period gives a hint of other hamlets and places in the parish now completely lost. Just before the Norman Conquest the Priory of Rochester received tithes of the manor of 'Bethencourt', the lands of which were said to have been owned by one Henry of Hoo Wolfward of the district. Later when the post reformation Dean and Chapter of Rochester leased these tithes they still carefully referred to them as being attached to Monken Barn at Thong in Shorne, and to be due out of lands in Shorne, Chalk and Henhurst in Cobham as part of the manor of Bethencourt, and in the early nineteenth century a map was prepared showing the lands involved, from which we find that the 'Manor' comprised a compact area containing the whole of the hamlet of Thong, with its surrounding lands from Clay Lane Woods in the west to Harts Hills between Thong and Shorne Ifield on the east. Monken Barn was on the west side of Thong Lane, north of what is now White Horse House. We leave this account of the lost Anglo Saxon places in the district with the thought that the 'Wolfward' accounts for the ditch and stockade around the ancient village of Merston.

Yet with all these names faded from the period, Shorne is not recorded. Indeed, when the Normans came and compiled their Domesday Book, Shorne was not named. The manors of Higham, Merston, Bickley, Chalk, Milton and Gravesend were all held by the Conqueror's half brother, the Bishop of Bayeux, and one 'Adam' is recorded as holding from the Bishop the block of manors Chalk, Bickley, and Higham. Nowhere is Shorne named.

Since the village with its Saxon name is clearly of Saxon origin, the absence of the village from what is often thought to be the complete Norman gazetteer needs explanation. Shorne's immediate neighbour to the east, Higham, is notable in Domesday for two reasons. It is easily the largest Domesday manor in the district, and Domesday says it was formerly two manors. It also had a fishery worth three shillings which was almost certainly based on the old 'Merscfleot'. For some reason best known to those who compiled Domesday it seems Shorne was at this time amalgamated with Higham.

Whether this explanation is correct, by the first half of the twelfth century the Manors of Higham and Shorne were in the king's hands and written records of Shorne survive.

1. Arch Cant., Vol.XXIV, page 86 and Vol.LXXXV, page 226.
2. Hasted, Vol.3, page 482, quoting Dio Cassius.
   Arch Cant., Vol.92, page 119, paper by Patrick Thornhill BA.
3. Gentleman's Magazine 1846, quoted in Collectaena Cantiana, G. Payne, page 150.
4. J.C. Wallenberg in his 'Place Names of Kent' suggests that the name is derived from the Anglo Saxon word 'Scoren' – to cut.
5. Arch. Cant., Vol.LV, page 14.
6. Said to be Text Roff. C105 and Reg Roff. 122/87.

The Church of Ss. Peter and Paul, Shorne, from the west, showing banded flint and ragstone of south aisle.

The church interior showing the north arcade with its various architectural styles, including Saxon double splay clerestory aperture over transitional style arch. Note lancet window in north aisle.

## Chapter 2
## THE EARLY CHURCH AND MANOR

In 1132 Henry I granted the church of Shorne and its tithes of corn and lambs, with the chapel of Cobham appendant, to the Monastery of St Saviour Bermondsey.[1] Even today this grant leaves its mark on the living which is a vicarage not a rectory. At first the monastery appointed casual priests to attend to the spiritual welfare of the parish, but after many years of litigation with the Bishops of Rochester about the bishop's right of supervision over the living, the monastery finally accepted in 1270 that the living should be a perpetual vicarage, the vicar to have the small tithes (such things as eggs and vegetables) and be responsible to the bishop, whilst the monks retained the right of presentation and the great tithes of corn and lambs.

Though there is no record of the church's foundation or its dedication to SS Peter and Paul, there is no doubt that it is of pre-conquest origin. It is mentioned in a list of chrism fees in the Rochester archives, which is usually considered to indicate a pre-conquest origin, and the building itself contains traces of Saxon workmanship. There is a small double splay window in the northern arcade of the nave which has survived the changes and chances of some nine centuries, whilst the round headed eastern arch in the same northern arcade (though too plastered over to permit examination of the workmanship) has Saxon rather than Norman proportions. Foundations of a wall running north from the western side of the arch have been found under the north aisle, which suggest a small transept or porticos into which the Saxon arch once gave access.

So we may assume that when the monks came to take possession of their royal gift they found a small stone built church with high double splayed clerestory windows lighting the nave, a small transept or side chapel on the north side and probably a small square chancel, which formed the basis of our present church.

Because of the uncertain status of the priests of the parish before the creation of the perpetual vicarage our information about the early vicars of the parish is slight. Between a casual reference to the king's chaplain Thurstin in the original grant by the king to the monastery and the final settlement with the Bishop of Rochester, a solitary record survives which illustrates the poverty of the living. An entry in the Close Rolls records that in 1269 one Robert 'Vicar of Shorne' was indebted to 'Master Jacob Son of Mosseus the Jew' for ten marks. One hopes that the 'perpetual vicarage' improved the vicar's living. In the event, after the appointment of one Nicholas in 1274 we have a long, though perhaps incomplete, list of vicars of the parish from that time.[2]

The fact that the church was in the gift of King Henry I in 1132 indicates that the manor was then royal demesne. Before Henry II died, however, the manor had passed into the hands of the de Nevill family. The exact date or terms of the grant of the manor appear to be unrecorded, but by a charter dated in 1208 King John granted to one Roger Canwell the remainder of certain rents reserved out of the Manor of Shorne 'which Henry II had given to Jolan de Nevill' and later King John confirmed to Jolan de Nevill the land in Shorne which King Richard had given him for one knight's fee.

Thus by the end of the twelfth century the church and the manor, two key elements in village history, have moved into focus. We have speculated about the church when the monks took it into their hands, but details of the manor, apart from a suggestion that the probable site of the manor house and demesne lands was in the area to the east of the Street, the manor house probably being sited where there are now three shops, we must leave any description of the manor to such items of manorial information which survive in much later records.

On the other hand, the story of the lords of the manor in medieval times is fairly complete, and so whilst we can trace the origins and development of the church from the fabric itself, we can only deal with the manor from the succession of lords through whose hands it passed.

The conjunction of the monastery and the manorial lords at the end of the twelfth century may well account for the first of the many alterations and enlargements of the church which took place during the next four centuries. By the end of the twelfth century the simple Saxon structure had been enlarged by the construction of a north aisle and a north chancel, whilst the chancel itself was greatly enlarged. The Saxon side chapel was used as the basis of the narrow north aisle and chancel, by cutting through its east and west walls to form arches, one of which leading into the north chancel is still extant, whilst the other seems to have been embellished with rounded half pillars, only the southern half pillar now surviving. The original Saxon arch into the old side chapel was left, whilst an arch was cut through the northern wall of the old nave beneath the clerestory windows to form with the original Saxon arch an arcade of two arches between the old nave and the new north aisle. The clerestory windows seemingly were left untouched to look out over the lean-to roof of the new aisle.

The evidence of enlargement of the chancel at this time is slight but convincing. The original Saxon chancel seems almost certainly to have been only about a third of the length of the present chancel, and there are indications of footings of a wall across the chancel at this point in the present chancel. There are several indications of the alteration and its probable date. The exterior of the present east wall of the chancel is of similar construction to that of the western wall of the north aisle, which is securely dated to the twelfth century by the narrow lancet window still in that wall. Both the aisle wall and the chancel wall have the only surviving traces of plastering on the church walls, which suggests their common time of construction. Inside the chancel the east wall has a battered and broken string course of apparently late twelfth century style which, though associated with the equally battered stonework of the aumbry in the east wall, has no apparent connection with the present arcades of the eastern part of the chancel. The chancel arch leading to the nave also seems to belong to this early period so far as its lower courses are concerned, being carved with dog tooth ornamentation much older than the remainder of the chancel arch. It seems probable that the monastery as the rector of the parish followed the common practice of the monastic orders of enlarging the chancels of the churches with which they were endowed, whilst perhaps the de Nevills, the new lords of the manor, added the north aisle and chancel on the side of the church nearest to their manor house in the Street.

From the thirteenth century onwards the tale of the lords of the manor is continuous. Jolan de Nevill, lord in 1199, was a clerk of the Exchequer and had two sons, John and Jolan. He died in 1207 and was succeeded by his eldest son, John, who was a soldier and saw service in Gascony. John had no children and on his death in 1220 the manor passed to his brother Jolan as is recorded by an entry in the Fine Rolls of the fourth year of Henry III.

Like his father Jolan the second was a judge who gained some eminence and was a Justice at Westminster when he died. He is said to be the author of 'Testa de Neville', an account of fees, sergeantries, etc, a well known work in its day. He also had extensive estates in Yorkshire, Lincolnshire and Nottinghamshire.[3]

Like many magnates at that time, and later, de Nevill was careful to acquire any further emoluments for his manor courts which might come his way. Shamwell hundred was then held by the Knights Templars by some earlier grant from the Crown. Custom required the tenants of all manors within the hundred, even the lord of the manor himself by his senechal or bailiff, to attend and do suit at the hundred courts at Michaelmas and Hocktide, a liability which accorded ill with the growing theory of manorial supremacy. Even more important probably was the fact that fines and fees of the hundred paid by the manorial tenants were taken by the Knights Templars, which no doubt de Nevill considered would be better in his pocket. So we find a record of a 'Fine'[4] which marks additions to the powers of the lords of Shorne Manor to the detriment of the hundred.

By this 'Fine' crimes committed within the manor either by tenants or strangers who were not tenants of the Knights Templars were to be heard in the manor courts and the lord of Shorne was to have the Assize of Bread and Ale and of Pillory and Tumbril in his manor. It may be mentioned that later the hundred itself passed into the hands of the de Cobham family and when centuries later the manor of Shorne came into their hands, by some strange confusion of legal forces the hundred and the Shorne manor courts were combined.

Though de Nevill's principal estates were by now mainly in the north he probably used the manor as a place of residence whilst performing his judicial duties at Westminster and he and his affairs were well known to the tenants of the manor. So on his death the usual Inquisition Post Mortem proceedings record.[5]

'John de Grene, John de Dunlege, William de Tumberwood, Adam de Pules, Roger de Tumberwood, Phillip de Merston, Henry de Lamare, Geoffrey le Fugal, Christopher de Sorene, Henry de la Hoke, Jordon de Breune, Hugh le Son, Henry de Sorene, Thomas Smallman and Sefan de Sorene, say on oath that Jolan de Nebill held of the King in Sorene 20 librates of land in capita by service of one knight's fee. They say also that one Jolan son of the said Jolan is his next heir and of age 22 years and a half."

Here is a list of tenants of the manor preserving some place names in the manor. John de Grene was clearly associated with the area still occupied by the present Green Farm in Lower Shorne, a place later to be associated with Merston as the manor of Merston and Green. The two men of Tumberwood came from a shadowy locality in Lower Shorne or Chalk which from time to time appears in medieval records. Phillip de Merston was clearly a neighbour of John de Green. So for a moment local names and people gain a fleeting record.

The third Jolan was still lord of the manor in 1254 when an assessment of knights' fees was made, but not long afterwards the manor passed into the hands of Roger de Northwood. The details of the transaction are obscured by an article in Archaeologia Cantiana Vol.II which gives what appear to be two versions. In one it says that de Nevill leased the manor to de Northwood, in another it says that the manor was leased to one John de Waltham, whose heiress Bonofilia de Waltham married Roger de Northwood. To add to the confusion Hasted says that the manor was granted by way of gift to de Northwood. The Charter Rolls however differ entirely from all this and record that in 1270 John de Nevill son of Jolan de Nevill granted and confirmed to Roger de Northwood for 350 silver marks, his manor of Shorne and two dowries issuing thereout, Roger de Northwood rendering to the said John and his heirs every year at Easter one pair of white gloves of the value of one penny in the churchyard of the same vill for all services.[6]

The explanation of this confusion is probably that the manor was indeed leased by de Nevill to John de Waltham in 1268 and that de Northwood married Bonofilia, his daughter and heir. The de Nevill lands were mostly in the north and, with the death of Jolan, his son John found himself with a manor which had been leased to de Waltham and was subject to two dowries, those of his grandmother and his mother. So a deal was arranged whereby John de Nevill granted the manor to Roger de Northwood, subject to the lease and the encumbering dowries for the good round sum of 350 silver marks. The grant, it should be noticed, was by subinfeudation. John de Nevill still held of the king and de Northwood held of de Nevill for the service of a pair of white gloves annually.

The de Northwood family, like the de Nevills, was founded upon the quill rather than the sword. Roger de Northwood, whose principal lands were in the Isle of Sheppey, was a baron of the Exchequer from 1274 until his death in 1285, and in 1277 was excused military service on account of his judicial duties.[7] In 1258 he was named as executor of Reginald de Cobham's will and this may have been the occasion of his first association with the district, where there were large de Cobham estates.

Like the earlier legal de Nevill, the legal de Northwood was keen to improve the profits of his fee. The year after he purchased he obtained a royal charter[8] to hold a market at the manor on Thursday in every week and a fair there every year to last three days on the vigil, the day, and the morrow of SS Peter and Paul, that is the 28th, 29th and 30th June, the saints being the patron saints of Shorne church. It is hard to imagine the weekly market, or the annual fair, bringing in much in the way of dues to the new lord, but the right of market was a fashionable appendage to a manor in those days and the grant marked the superiority of Shorne over other manors in or around the parish. A little later the usual Quo Warranto proceedings, which Edward I used to check manorial pretensions, conceded that Roger de Northwood had a right of warren in the manor. Probably the southern side of Barrow Hill, still known as the Warren, was the site of the manorial warren in 1291.

Not long after this Roger de Northwood died. His son, John, like John de Nevill a century before, was a soldier. He seems to have been successful in his career and managed to squeeze out the picturesque but plebian socage tenure with its service of a pair of white gloves, by holding the manor direct from the king for the glories of Grand Sergeantry, the service being to carry a white banner before the king for forty days in the king's wars with Scotland.[9] This duty was to prove onerous, it being recorded that John de Northwood served in Scotland in the years 1309, 1311, 1314 and 1318. Probably he saw little of his Shorne manor, for he was a man of some importance. Besides his service in Scotland, he served in France and Flanders. At home he was Sherriff of Kent, Conservator of the Peace, Commissioner of Bridges, on the commission of Oyer and Terminer and Supervisor of the army of Kent. In the struggle between Edward II and the barons, John de Northwood was one of the 'Majores Barons'.[10]

At this point it is convenient to leave the manor of Shorne and glance at adjoining manors and other medieval matters affecting the parish during the late thirteenth and fourteenth centuries.

1. Hasted, Vol.III, page 452.
2. Fieldings Records of Rochester.
3. Dict. Nat. Biog.
4. Kent Records, Vol.XV, Calendar of Kent Fees of Fines, page 143.
5. Arch Cant., Vol.II.
6. Cal. Charter Rolls, 54, Hen.III.
7. Dict. Nat. Biog.
8. Cal. Charter Rolls, 59, Hen.III.
9. Hasted gets the tenure wrong, legally is was not knights service.
10. Dict. Nat. Biog.

The roof timbers of the central aisle of the church, showing the king posts now concealed by the ceiling.

An old photograph of the interior of the church before the present chancel screen was erected.

## Chapter 3
## OTHER MANORS AND A MEDIEVAL MYSTERY

It is generally accepted that Meleston, a manor mentioned in Domesday, is the Saxon village of Merscton which by medieval times was known as Merston. In Domesday it is said to have land for one plough, with five villeins, and it seems to have never been more than the area of about 150 acres which the tithe map of 1842 shows as the parish of Merston. At the time the de Northwoods were lords of Shorne, Merston was held by Robert de Sancto Clare as one knight's fee. It was one of the vills of the Hundred of Shamwell and had a church dedicated to St Giles.

What Merston was like at the beginning of the fourteenth century is hard to visualise. Doubtless the ancient ditch round the vill was but a shadow of the Saxon stockaded entrenchment. From its excavated foundations the church was a small Norman building about 53 feet long with a curved apse at the eastern end and a small tower at its western end. A fourteenth century coffin slab has been ploughed out of the church site, but its original place in the church cannot now be determined. Crop marks a few yards south of the church suggest another building and earlier antiquarians have reported there was a deep draw well to the south east of the church of which there is now no sign.

It seems that Merston suffered during the Black Death. There are records of two rectors being appointed in 1349 and another the following year. Whether the plague caused the complete depopulation of the village or not, by 1455 the place was uninhabited. In that year the Bishop of Rochester, after appointing one John Hedon to be the rector, recorded that the living was only worth thirty shillings, that there was no parsonage house or manor house and no inhabitants of the parish. He therefore licensed John Hedon to live elsewhere on condition that he kept the church in repair and celebrated mass there on the festival of St Giles each year.

This appears to be the first record of the complete depopulation of the village and it may be that other events besides pestilence completed what the Black Death had begun. At the beginning of the fifteenth century the manor passed into the hands of one John Smyth, who is said to have been a prosperous London fishmonger. At that time there was much clearing of land and villages to put them down to grass for sheep grazing, so perhaps the city speculator, and not the plague, caused the final clearance of the village of which no trace now shows above the surface of the fields of Green Farm. John Smyth was buried at Shorne and had a small brass there, most of which has now unfortunately vanished.

It seems that successive rectors faithfully discharged their duty of repairing the church. When the site was excavated the debris contained a large number of roof tiles which appeared to be of two varieties, suggesting that the church was tiled at an early date and then repaired at least once before its final decay. Mass at the church fell into abeyance at the Reformation and the building decayed during the seventeenth and eighteenth centuries, the last ruins being reported to be in a small wood. The village has a story that most of its flint walls were robbed for flint knappers and for flints for the walls around Court Lodge in Shorne. Nineteenth century sinecure rectors of the parish tried to revive the annual service on St Giles day, but it seems they completely missed the site, which by then was under plough, and held their services in a small wood about a quarter of a mile from the true site.

Whilst the ancient Saxon village of Merston was falling into decay a notable manor — but it was never more than a manor — grew within the parish boundaries. The manor of Randall, Roundal or Rundale — the spellings vary — was not a revival of one of the ancient shadowy manors which we have mentioned as existing in and around the parish at the end of the Saxon period. The de Cobham family already mentioned in this history, from early times had held lands in Shorne. In 1287 John de Cobham died and his two sons John and Henry divided his estates between them.[1]

The manor of Randall in Shorne fell to the share of Henry (who was to become commonly known as 'le eine' — the uncle — to distinguish him from his nephew Henry son of John) whilst John took lands in Cobham and Cooling. This is the first occasion which can be traced when the manor of Randall is named and its origin is obscure. From an extent of the manor dated in the early fourteenth century it seems the manor was a conglomoration consisting of a subinfeudation from the Abbess of Fontevrand at forty pence a year, a similar holding from one Edmund de Pakenham at seven shillings a year and the remainder, some 120 acres of arable land 20 acres of pasture, 5 acres of wood, 80 acres of saltmarsh and a windmill, was held of Roger de Northwood by the service of thirty-five shillings a year, obviously a subinfeudation of part of Shorne manor. The reference to a windmill is interesting and raises the query whether this was in fact the Shorne windmill which is mentioned in an extent of Shorne manor of about the same date. Two windmills within a limited area at so early a period seem unlikely. Probably the manor of Shorne relied on its watermill in Shorne Street about which we have to tell later.

Notwithstanding its scrappy origin when Henry 'le eine' acquired the manor of Randall he made it his home in a fashion very different from the lords of Shorne and for a couple of generations Randall was a famous manor house from which members of the de Cobham family rode forth as sheriffs, knights of the shire, lords of parliament, or to join the king's array.

The manor house has now disappeared, but the site is identifiable. Weever writing in 1631 says that in his day 'scarce the ruins appear to direct where the house stood . . .' Today the traces are even more gone in decay. Under a tangle of roots and coppice woodland, traces of the old building show that it had substantial stone foundations standing on a rectangular plateau surrounded on three sides by a moat and fishponds. Lying in a valley on the north side of Randall Heath, it was protected to the south and west by the high ground of the heath and looked out to the north over the fishpond (about half an acre) to a distant view of the Thames. Excavations on the site show signs that it was probably on the site of an earlier building, the rebuilding being probably late thirteenth or early fourteenth century. A feature of the walls is that the angles are founded upon large sarsen stones. The remains of a large medieval hearth consisting of a large flat sarsen stone surrounded by tiles set on edge was also found.

The life of 'le eine' was an epitome of the life of a knight of the times. He married a rich heiress in the person of Joan, daughter of Stephen de Penchester, through whom he acquired Allington Castle and other estates. He was elected as knight of the shire in 1307. Royal favour was gained, it is said, as the result of his personal bravery in the wars of King Edward I with the Welsh and Scots, and he is said to have been made a knight banneret in the field for gallantry at the seige of Calaverock in Scotland in 1300.[2] Following this he was sheriff of Kent in 1301, 1302, 1307 and 1315. Upon the death of Edward I (unlike his neighbour de Northwood) he seems to have supported Edward II against the barons and probably because of this loyalty he was created Lord of Randall and received a writ of summons to the Lords in the year before his death.

Though travelling far in the service of the king, and although he had a castle at Allington, Randall seems to have been his main home and, for the first time in this history, it is possible to trace a close connection between a local magnate and the village in which he had an estate. During his lifetime he built Randall Chapel (now the south chancel) at Shorne Church and his effigy as Lord of Randall still rests 'armed in mail and crosslegged' in the rebuilt chapel. On the tomb is an inscription said to be a modern copy of the original

> 'Sir Henri de Cobham le eine seignour de Roundale fust apele gist ley dieu de salme et merci'

The helmet on which the effigy's head rests is remarkable as having its interior carefully carved to show the method of fitting and padding the helmet, not unlike the padding of a modern crash helmet.

On the death of 'le eine' his son, Sir Stephen, succeeded to the barony and for something like a hundred years the manor was to be an important part of the life of the village, though after a couple of generations it was usually occupied by collaterals of the main line of the family. In 1368 Thomas Morice, a wealthy pleader in the Kings Courts, left to his son in law Sir Thomas de Cobham his leasehold interest in Randall and — a strange appurtenance for a lawyer — his armour.[3]

Before Sir Henry de Cobham had established his chapel, another building, in many ways one of the most mysterious in the parish, had been built near the glebe lands and tithe barn in Crown Lane, which were then part of the monastic holdings as rectors of Shorne. Now known as 'St Katherines' it is unquestionably an ecclesiastical building with a thirteenth century sedilia and from its architecture appears to have been built in the late thirteenth century with later alterations. In the grounds around the chapel are numerous burials found during excavations for foundations and drains of recent buildings. There is even what one might call the traditional story of a stone coffin having been found, though this was little more than hearsay even in the eighteenth century. Yet there is no record of the foundation of this chapel, who built it is unknown, as also those who altered it, whilst the purpose of the building has been the subject of much speculation.

The name 'St Katherines' is based upon the chance record of its final passing into lay hands long after the Reformation, when in 1581 a Commission of Concealed Lands reported that the chapel of St Katherine with a small croft or garden in Shorne worth 2d. per annum had been overlooked in the earlier turnover of church lands. No owner, ecclesiastical or lay, is mentioned in the finding and the property was vested in the Crown as part of its Manor of Greenwich and later sold into private hands.

There have been several suggestions as to the original purpose of the chapel. The fact that it was near the glebe and tithe barn suggests that it was originally connected in some way with the monastery of Bermondsey. Yet by the time of the suppression of the monasteries any such association must have been completely forgotten. The Crown had no difficulty in acquiring the lands and endowments of Bermondsey, including the rectorial tithes of Shorne and the tithe barn, which later passed from the Crown to the Dean and Chapter of Rochester. It has been suggested that the chapel was a chantry built by a manorial lord, but the only lords of manors nearby were de Northwood, who had his base at Sheppey, and Henry de Cobham, who built Randall Chapel at Shorne Church at about this time. The suggestion that it was a chapel of ease for the parishioners seems quite impossible with the church – an earlier foundation – only a few hundred yards to the south.

The most likely purpose seems to have been that of a pilgrim chapel. These chapels, in one form or another, are not uncommon in Kent on the pilgrim routes to Canterbury and are often associated with the passage of dangerous parts of the journey. For instance the bridge at Rochester had its chapel at which the wayfarer might offer his thanks to the saints at having crossed the then somewhat perilous bridge over the Medway.

This idea is supported by our knowledge of the scene at the time the chapel was built. By the middle of the thirteenth century there was a busy pilgrim traffic from London, and indeed all England, to Canterbury and the shrine of St Thomas. The first pilgrims travelled on the ancient line of the Roman road along the southern boundary of Shorne as is evidenced by St Thomas's Well near the junction of Thong Lane with the old road. By the end of the thirteenth century, however, an important secondary route had developed. The pilgrim or traveller could board a 'tide boat' at Billingsgate and take the 'long ferry' to Gravesend, thus saving much time and energy, and then set off from Gravesend to Rochester.

This undoubtedly introduced a new element into the village picture. Until the 'ferry' developed, the only traffic between Gravesend and Rochester was of necessity local traffic and the winding lanes between Gravesend, Milton next Gravesend, Denton, and Chalk were simple links between village communities. Beyond Chalk the road to Shorne slanted to the south at Deadman's bottom on the boundary between Chalk and Shorne, crossing what are now open fields to join Crown Lane near the tithe barn.[4] Beyond Shorne there were no further communities until one reached Strood, Higham village lying well to the north. From the Shorne villagers' point of view the most convenient route to Strood was over Shorne Ridgeway to the Three Crutches, where a triple cross stood, and thence to Strood. This route avoided the wilds of Gads Hill which stood in the waste hinterlands between Shorne and Strood at the northern end of Shorne Ridgeway. To the traveller desirous of using the most direct route to Rochester Bridge, however, there was a more or less straight road over the crest of Gads Hill.

With the development of the 'ferry' the long distance traveller and the pilgrim generally preferred the direct route, with the perils of robbery and violence for which the wastes of Gads Hill later became notorious. The old route to the village and then on passed the site of St Katherine's chapel, but the direct route to Gads Hill was only a couple of hundred yards to the north of the monastic lands. It seems probable that the priory, looking for some profit from the pilgrim traffic, built the chapel as a place where the traveller might make his prayer and offering for a safe journey or return to St Katherine, a travellers' protectress.

The obvious signs of alteration and restoration of the building in the following centuries suggest that the original builders of the chapel lost interest in it and that subsequent maintenance fell on others. In the fifteenth century there was an active guild of Corpus Christi in the parish. These guilds often undertook the maintenance of pious purposes within the parish in which they operated. Thus it seems possible that when the priory lost interest in the chapel, the village guild took over its maintenance for the benefit of the passing pilgrim and perhaps for the guild's own use. This would explain why at the dissolution of the monasteries the place was not included among the monastic possessions seized by the Crown.

The association of the chapel with pilgrims and travellers may account for the graves around the chapel. Later during the seventeenth and eighteenth centuries a constant feature of our burial registers is the death, under hedges, or wayside barns, of the wayfarer ('a stranger' he was usually called) who ended his or her travels within the parish bounds. So may the burials in the grounds of the old chapel represent the pilgrims who during the centuries of faith ended their pilgrimage in Shorne.

1 An indication that the lands were held on the tenure of gavelkind and not knight service, when primogeniture would have prevailed.
2 Arch. Cant. Vol. 22 page 203
3 Arch. Cant. Vol. XXIX page 157
4 See a map of C1712 in possession of the Rochester Bridge Wardens which clearly shows this road surviving into the eighteenth century.

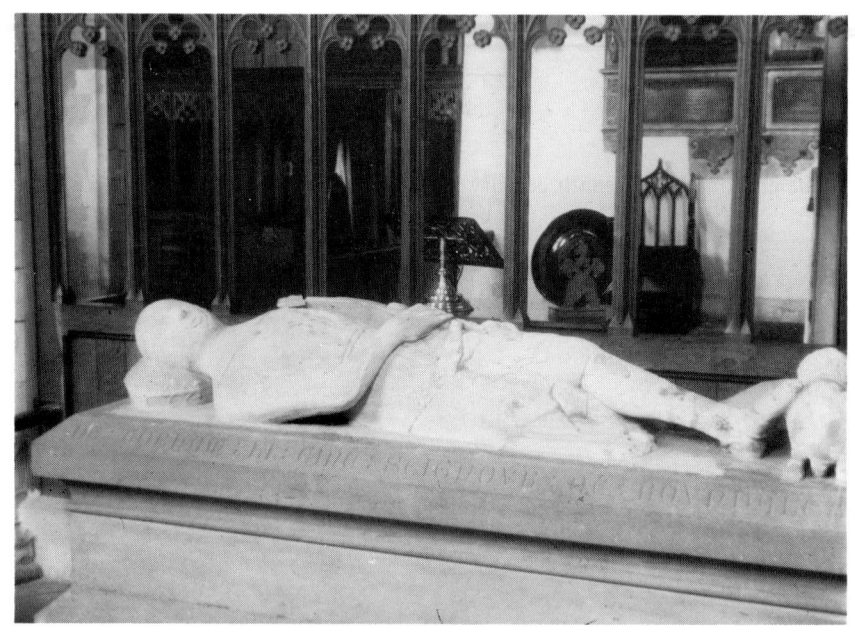

Sir Henry de Cobham, Lord of Randall, in the rebuilt Randall Chapel.

St Katherine's chapel from the west, showing the 15th century door.

## Chapter 4
## THE LATER MEDIEVAL CHURCH, MANOR, AND PEOPLE

The end of the thirteenth century marked the beginning of many alterations to the basically Saxon church building with its clerestory windows and twelfth century north aisle and enlarged chancel.

When Sir Henry de Cobham 'Lord of Randall' decided to build his chapel as an appurtenance to the church, it seems the monastery took advantage of his proposals. Their enlarged chancel was still a relatively simple structure with a blank wall apart from possible Early English windows on the south side and probably a heavy wall on the north side between the chancel and the north chancel, broken only by the western arch of the present arcade. The proposed chapel would in effect be a south chancel and the whole scheme gave an opportunity to open and lighten the whole eastern end of the main chancel. What arrangements were made between Sir Henry and the Priory we do not know, but as a result we now have the two fine early English bays at the eastern end of the chancel opening into Sir Henry's new chapel on the south side and the older north chancel opposite.

Probably this alteration to the chancel was accompanied by the heightening of the chancel arch into the nave. The original arch with its dog tooth ornamentation constructed on the earlier enlargement of the chancel was probably lower than the present lofty pointed arch, and the present workmanship of the upper part of the present arch resembles the workmanship of the plain masonry of the new arcades at the east end of the chancel.

The building of the Randall chapel was followed by the construction of the south aisle. We can only surmise the date of this enlargement of the main body of the church. The early English style of the Randall Chapel accords well enough with the life time of Sir Henry de Cobham who died about 1315 and was buried in his chapel with his effigy presiding over the chapel; but the arch leading from the Randall chapel into the south aisle and the south aisle itself were constructed in a rough 'decorated' style whilst the window at the western end of the south aisle is an example of 'decorated' tracery. It may be supposed that the building of the Randall Chapel suggested the idea of the south aisle, but by the time the construction was begun after the Randall Chapel was completed the builders chose the decorated style then coming into fashion rather than the, by then, old fashioned early English style of the Randall Chapel. The distinct difference between the fine masonry of the early English arches in the chancel and the coarse workmanship of the south aisle arcade of three arches suggests not only a difference in time, but also less wealthy builders.

During the fifteenth century the north wall of the north aisle was rebuilt, apparently on a line inside the line of the older wall, making the already narrow north aisle even narrower, and the nave and north aisle were reroofed, the old clerestory windows being covered by the new roof which is a continuous sweep of roof from the apex of the nave to the outer wall of the north aisle. The main part of the roof over the nave has four fine king posts of considerable size, obviously intended to be open to view though now concealed by a plaster ceiling.

Whilst these alterations were being made to the church, the manor was passing from father to son in the de Northwood family. Sir John Northwood was succeeded by a son, a grandson and a great grandson. The great grandson, Roger de Northwood, found himself in much the same position as his predecessors, the de Nevills, had been in when the original de Northwood acquired the manor — his inheritance encumbered with two dowries in favour of his mother and grandmother. There is the usual confusion of records. In 1393 there is a record of a royal pardon to de Northwood for having granted the manor to trustees without royal license, and then shortly after another royal pardon to Arnold Savage ('the King's Knight' he is called, he was also Speaker of the House of Commons) for having acquired the manor from Sir Roger. Probably all this was part of the complicated legal formalities of those days and by 1407 Sir Arnold Savage of Bobbing was the lord of Shorne manor.

The passing of the manor into the hands of a new family seems always to have been the signal for some legal or technical changes in the manor or its customs. The sale to Sir Arnold Savage was no exception.

In the Close Rolls[1] is enrolled an agreement between the new lord of the manor and his tenants, and with the enrolment much of the medieval manor, the knight's fee of the de Nevills, the pride of the de Northwoods with the white banner before the king in the Scottish wars, changed into the economic manor with quit rents and customs which were to continue in a recognisable form for another four hundred years.

The agreement was between Sir Arnold Savage and fifty one named tenants of the manor ranging from Sir John Cobham, Lord of Cobham, Sir William Tanner, Master of Cobham College of Chantry Priests, and Thomas, son and heir of Sir Reynold Cobham of Randale, to otherwise unknown individuals (all of whom are proudly stated to be freeholders of the manor — there was no serfdom in Kent). It contains many important recitals which enable us to glimpse something of the ancient life of the old manor, its customs and topography.

The tenants are stated to be of the 'Northborg' and 'Southborg' of the manor. The agreement recites that the tenants of the 'Southborg' possessed altogether 516½ acres and 6½ dayworks of land and the common of pasture thereout for 310 sheep upon the lord's soil in Shornewood.

The services for their land were complicated. In autumn the tenants were bound to reap wheat, rye or oats in 77½ acres of the lord's demesne. They also had to perform three works for every ten acres held, two of the 'works' being called 'Shefwork' and the other 'Herdwerk'. For the 'Shefwerk' they took two sheaves of corn, but if they did not do the work they paid 5d. per shefwerk. For every 'Herdwerk' not performed they were fined 6d. Again for every ten acres they held they were liable to thresh one quarter of wheat or pay 4d. and likewise carry one quarter of corn from the manor barn to the ship in Shornefleet, or pay 1d. at the choice of the lord. Again for every ten acres they had to hoe for half a day in the lord's corn or pay 1d. at the choice of the lord. Two small levies of ¾d., for 'medesilver', and ¼d., for 'Stubblewerk', were also attached to each ten acres, and there was a further requirement to make an enclosure about the manor court of 25½ perches, 5 feet of walls. View of Frankpledge held at Michaelmas and Easter supervised all this and at those courts two of the tenants were chosen for the office of reeve and bedel of whom the lord chose one, and a common fine of 20s. was levied each half year.

The tenantry claimed that all this was exceedingly burdensome and 'for the sake of peace' 'by unanimous accord' the lord granted to the tenants quittance from these services in exchange for the tenants giving up their rights of common pasture over Shornewood and the tenants of the Southborg paying a total rent of 73s.2d. at St Peter's chains for all their land at the rate of 17d. per ten acres. So passed the ancient services of shefwerk, herdwerk, hoeing, threshing and carting, which from the days of the Conquest at least had in their unrecorded seasonal and never ending routine maintained the manorial structure.

The agreement saved all other services to the lord, and indeed from later records it is clear that it did not cover all aspects of manorial life. For instance the acreage of the Northborg is not specified and, though the agreement might be interpreted as dealing with the manorial services of both 'Borgs', it is clear from later manor rolls that the Northborg also commuted services for quit rents at some time or other, since the later manor rolls appear to cover about nine hundred acres of land with quit rents totalling over £13 a year. Likewise the agreement makes no mention of the common grazing on Shorne Mead, which was not finally enclosed until the nineteenth century, whilst eighteenth century manor rolls record the appointment of manorial officers, the borseholder, the aletaster and the hayward, who are not mentioned in the fifteenth century agreement. Of all the services mentioned in the agreements, the most interesting is the service of carrying the lord's corn from his manor barn to his ship in Shornefleet. Here is evidence of the continuance of this ancient 'Fleot' of Roman and Saxon times, and perhaps we may make a short digression from the manor to what is known about this now completely vanished harbour.

Rather over a century before the manorial agreement of 1407 the ancient ferry to Essex from Higham, using this creek, formed part of the endowments of the Higham Priory of Nuns, which in 1292 was presented at the Assizes for allowing the bridge and causeway to the ferry to be broken. At the same time the boatmen on the ferry were presented for overcharging – a common complaint against ferrymen. The Prioress pleaded that the damage to the causeway arose from inundation, apparently a sudden surge rather than a slow rise in river levels. The Priory then repaired the causeway and maintained the 'bridge', having a period of relative prosperity during the fourteenth century, suggesting that the ferry was contributing profitably to the monastic income.

The Page Memorial in the chancel: George Page on the left in sober garb, Sir William Page on the right in half armour and Elizabethan trimmings. Each is supported by his wife, the lady on the left being Lady Eleanor Page who erected the memorial.

It is interesting to glance at the evidence of changing marsh levels during the medieval and later centuries. In the early thirteenth century Hasted records an old deed of grant by de Nevill to Henry Cobham of a meadow called Boleham Meadow. By the time John de Cobham was founding his chantry of priests in the fourteenth century this had become Boleham Marshes and, at the beginning of the seventeenth century, the parish rate accounts refer to some eighty acres of marsh land known as Bulham Salts.

Today a visit to the site makes it hard to believe that this was ever an effective harbour, but a map in the Darnley collection dated 1759 shows that even as late as the eighteenth century the creek was still open to the river. It is generally accepted that much of the Thameside marshes were embanked in the fourteenth/fifteenth centuries, but the Darnley map shows that the present stretch of river wall between Shorne Mead fort and Cliffe Creek was not in existence in the eighteenth century and that the whole creek, with a considerable area of saltings, was embanked by a wall from the river at Shorne Mead to the slightly higher ground around Bickley and Higham Church, and by the Higham causeway from

Bickley back to the river bank. The possible date of the final closing of the creek is suggested as early nineteenth century because as late as 1811 the overseers of Shorne relieved one J. Butler with £2 'To repair his boat', suggesting that there was still some use of the creek at this time.

That the creek was used by other craft, and fishermen, as well as the ferry to East Tilbury in the late medieval period is suggested by one or two fragments of information which survive. In 1349, for instance, the Sheriff of Kent was ordered to arrest one Peter Elys of Shorne who had been chosen by one Adam Cooper master of a ship called 'La Laurence' under a commission of the Crown as a fit mariner for the king's service. Peter Elys had apparently been 'pressed' and escaped. 'A fit mariner' suggests he was a seaman — probably a fisherman — and not some country bumpkin. Again the use of the creek as a fisherman's haven would explain why two of the more prominant villagers in that period, Stephen Alleyn and John Smythe, were reputed to be members of the Fishmongers Company. It is not unlikely that John de Rede of Shorne, who in 1325 acknowledged his indebtedness to Stephen Alleyne, was a fisherman.

The list of fifty-one tenants of the manor is of interest if we compare it with two other lists of names of villagers which have survived; the Lay Subsidy Roll of 1334/5 and the list of rebels pardoned after the Jack Cade rebellion in 1450.

The Lay Subsidy Roll lists the names under the heading of hundreds, but when we find a reference to Jas-atte-Regway and in the next fifty names, names like Widow Thurston att-Regway, Lady de Rundale and Roger de Northwood we can assume that this is the Shorne part of the list. Amongst these names (besides one William Tumberwood who must have been a descendant of William or Roger Tumberwood the jurymen at the Inquisition Post Mortem of Jolan de Nevill a hundred years before) there are twelve names in the Subsidy Roll which can be associated with names in the list of tenants of the manor some seventy years later.

Most of course are but names, for instance William Rolf of the 1345 list must have been an ancestor of John Rollf, a tenant of the manor in 1407, but of some of the others we find other records. For instance the 1345 list has a number of 'Atte-Pettes': John, Henry, Peter and Alice. All paid subsidies: Peter, the wealthiest, paying 10s. The only other local people paying a comparable subsidy were Lady de Rundale, and Sir Roger de Northwood. Peter Atte-Pette's wealth is confirmed in the Close Rolls, where in 1344 it is recorded that Gilbert Godwyne of Rochester owed Peter Atte-Pette the sum of £21. In 1347 it is also recorded that Peter Atte-Pette of Shorne 'the Elder' was to appear before the council to answer charges. In the list of the manor tenants, we find William atte-Pette, obviously a descendant of Peter or one of the other Pettes of the earlier record.

Turning to the list of pardoned rebels of 1450, though there are no longer any Pettes or Rolfs (they may not have been rebels) there are several whose names appear in the manor tenantry. Richard Vesey of the manor list was either the Richard Vesey pardoned in 1450 or his father. William Newman recorded in 1407 may have been the father of Richard Newman pardoned in 1450. The

Smythe family appears in the manor tenantry and the list of pardoned and this family left a fragment of brass memorial in the church.

Two names however justify further examination. In all three lists the names of Davy and Hawkes appear. John Davy in the Subsidy Roll paid 9¾d., one of the smallest amounts in the list. In the list of tenants of the manor was Thomas Davy, and amongst those pardoned for rebellion was John Davy. Other records of the Davy family occur. There is an undated legacy recorded in Thorpe's Customale Roffensis whereby Thomas Davy bequeathed a cade of red herrings and half a cade of white herrings to be distributed amongst the poor of Shorne on the Wednesday before Passion Sunday in every year and also gave a little house in Shorne 'besides the tenement of Masons' which he had purchased from Richard Stevens, as an almshouse to continue and abide for ever. To support the gift of herrings he charged ten acres of land in Merston. Thomas Davy with his lands in Merston and his little house near Masons had come a long way from his ancestor who had only paid a 9¾d. subsidy.

The Hawkes family were equally well established in the village. John is named in the Subsidy Roll, Robert in the manor tenantry, and another John in the list of rebels. John Hawkes only paid 8½d. subsidy, but by the fifteenth century the family were benefactors of the church, and by the sixteenth century substantial landowners. Richard Hawkes who died in 1473, desired to be buried in the south part of the church and gave legacies (including one to the Light of Corpus Christi). In 1497 John Hawkes died and left two bushels of barley to the Rood of Rest in the church, and six shillings and eight pence towards the buying of the great bell. Later still in the 1598 poor law accounts Reginald Hawkes was rated for 420 acres. He died in 1600 and for some years thereafter the parish received from Dudley Hawkes ten shillings a year for the poor under his will. Thus we can trace this family through some two hundred and fifty years of village history — an unprecedented period which no other family in the village can match. Yet by the end of the second decade of the sixteenth century all trace of this family vanishes from the parish records.

1. Cal. Close Rolls, Henry IV, Vol.III, page 388.

## Chapter 5
## MEDIEVAL EPILOGUE

In the Fifteenth century the status of the vicar seems to have improved, and in 1452 William Pepyr becomes the first vicar of whom we know more than his name. He was also vicar of Chalk, and held both livings until his death in 1468, when he was buried on the south side of the chancel as directed by his will. A mutilated stone from which the brass has long since been lost still marks his last resting place. He seems to have been a man of some learning and wealth for by his will he not only bequeathed to the parish a 'vicarage house', but also his book 'The Golden Legend' to his successors at Shorne to remain in the church (it is now long lost), and then gave another book called 'Pupila Oculi' to one William Sanders.

He also had the temerity to try to extract additional stipend from the Abbey. The story of his battle with the Abbey of Bermondsey is recorded in a wordy petition to the bishop by his successor John Pegion, a copy of which survives amongst the diocesan records. According to this petition William Pepyr appealed to the ecclesiastical authorities for some relief because the parish of Shorne was 'large, laboursome and of great extent' and the 'Porcon of the said vicar . . . is insufficient, and not able to sustain him in his duties'. He also complained that he 'was constrained for lack of a vicarage to buy him a little ground at his cost and build the same to his great cost'. All this, and much more, was poured into the ear of authority, which ordered the Monastery to augment the vicar's income by ten marks a year out of its appropriated tithes, and to repair the vicarage house 'once'. Despite this order the Abbey 'dishonestly of malice apelid to the Courte of Roame'. Even Rome was against the Abbey and remitted the matter back to the English Court for execution. Still the Abbey delayed and William Pepyr died without receiving anything. John Pegion the petitioner prayed that he might have execution against the Abbey.

The story ends at this point and we do not know what success John Pegion had with his petition. There is a licence in the papal registers permitting John Pegion to hold livings in plurality, which was after all, what William Pepyr had done. Perhaps this was a compromise which ended the matter.

The vicarage built by William Pepyr is one of the minor mysteries of parochial history. By his will he bequeathed it to the church of Shorne and presumably John Pegion lived in this vicarage. Only two years after John Pegion died, however, Thomas Page (one of the small local squires) made his will, whose provisions suggest that William Pepyr's vicarage had already been lost to the parish, perhaps because of the weakness of ecclesiastical authority in its control of parochial property. The whole bequest is worth repeating:—

'I will that my feoffee make or deliver a state unto Sir Thomas Elis nowe vicar of Shorne, and to x or xii of the beste disposed younge men of the parishe of Shorne in a tenement callid Normans lying and sityng in Up Shorn in the said parishe to have and to holde to them their heires and assignes for ever to the entent that they shall suffer the be for named Sir Thomas Elis vicar of the same parishe to have and to occupie the saide tenement as the vicars dwellyng place as long as he livith and ther continueth vicar and yiff the saide Sir Thomas decesses or be promotid to any other benyfices there not being vicar then the said tenement to remain to the vicar nexte succeedyng him in lyke form as hit ys grauntid to the same Sir Thomas and so the tenement to be contynued fro vicar to vicar in lyke forme as longe as the world shall endure provided all waye that the saide Sir Thomas and his successours shall yerely saye or do to saye on the Ascension daye placebo and dirige wt comendacon and masse on the morowe following in the churche of Shorn for the sowll of Thomas Page and his ansistres sowlls and all Xtien sowlles'.[1]

The old vicarage still stands on the corner of the Street opposite to the entrance of the church way. Its exterior and interior have been greatly altered from the days of Thomas Page by generations of vicars and parish officers (there are a number of entries in later parish records concerning repairs and alterations) and finally by the late George Matthews Arnold. He was a nineteenth century antiquary whom we shall meet again later in this story, and he removed ancient plaster covering the timber frames and added other embellishments. But its main timbers have outlived the fidelity of men, for the changes and chances of four hundred and fifty years have combined to defeat Thomas Page in every particular. No longer do Shorne vicars reside there 'fro vicar to vicar . . . as long as the worlde shall endure'; no longer are 'placebo and dirige with comendacon and masse on the morowe' said on Ascension day in Shorne church for the soul of Thomas Page; finally the 'old vicarage' which by the seventeenth century was known as the 'Cross House' having been occupied by successive parish clerks for over a century, was sold into private hands in 1895.

The timbers of the old vicarage remind us that the fifteenth century was the period of much building of fine timber framed houses, some of which have survived in the district. The most notable of these is the timber framed house now known as 'Little St Katherines' standing near St Katherine's chapel. It is a fine example of a Kentish yeoman's hall house which after being used as three cottages, has recently been restored. Its roof timbers still contain a small king post and are encrusted with the soot of the open fire which once burned in the hall. From the standard and style of the timber workmanship which has survived in this house one can realise the technical skill and sheer hard work which was needed to construct this type of house. Unhappily we do not know who built it nor who lived in it in the days of its early rugged comfort.

Another house in the village, now the post office, retains a timber frame of a similar house now enclosed in a brick case, probably added in the eighteenth century, whilst opposite the Post Office is Cobb Cottage, another timber framed house of perhaps a little later date. Similarly much ancient timber in the cottage opposite the church gate suggests that here was once another house, smaller than Little St Katherine's, but of similar construction.

We know little about the builders or occupiers of these houses, but it is worth remembering that these were all probably built in the fifteenth century after the enfranchisement of the manor tenants by the agreement with Arnold Savage. They are all within a quarter of a mile of each other and suggest a closely-knit community of yeomen who were well satisfied with the freedom given them by the new terms of the manor customs.

Something of the outlook of this community is afforded us by the two or three generations of parishioners who in the century before the Reformation made bequests for the benefit of the village and the church. Thomas Page's bequest of a vicarage was but one of a whole series of gifts recorded in those years which enable us to date with rather more precision than hitherto the last additions and alterations to the fabric of the church.

By its style the tower was built in the fifteenth century, and this is confirmed by a number of legacies all in the last decade of the fifteenth century which suggest that the new tower needed bells to complete its purpose. We do not know who paid for the erection of the tower but we know that in 1491 John Page gave a legacy 'for a nu bel'. In 1495 Thomas Page, in addition to giving the vicarage, also gave xls. 'to buying of a great bell', whilst in the following year Thomas Catter gave a further vjs. viijd. towards the 'great bell', as did John Hawke in the following year. The great bell however does not seem to have been a success as in 1521 Richard Creslake gave another vjs. viijd. 'to the amending of ye great bell of Shorne'.

Other structural changes in the church were made at about this time. Thomas Catter in his will in 1496 gave a legacy for the making of an arch in the church. This is almost certainly the western arch which completes the three bays in the south arcade of the chancel, which from its style is of this period. Likewise the great east window of the chancel is fifteenth century in style and probably replaced thirteenth century early English windows at the time the tower was finished.

Another important part of the furnishing of the church seems to have been constructed or rebuilt in the latter half of the fifteenth century. In 1468 Agnes Oxenham left a legacy of xiijs. ivd. to the making of the 'hye rode loft', and in 1487 William Chamber gave a legacy for the 'edefying of the rode loft'. John Page in 1491 gave vls. to the 'paynting of the new rode loft', a gift supported in 1496 by another legacy for the same purpose by Alexander Eversley. The only trace of this screen and loft today are two or three panels of the present chancel screen, which on its erection in 1902 incorporated parts of the lower portion of the old screen. This had survived as part of the pewing of the church in the

One of the sides of the octagonal font, showing the baptism of Christ, the Baptist using a jug.

seventeenth century. The Randall Chapel also has a rood screen which has survived from this time, having been constructed or restored by a legacy of William Walleyce in 1473.

The painting of the 'rode loft' reminds us that there was then much other colour in the church. One or two of the pillars in the south arcade of the nave bear hints of colour, whilst the corbels supporting the timber of the nave roof, with their shields, still show on close examination much colour beneath the coats of whitewash applied by succeeding generations. It may well be that these were the arms recorded by one of the old seventeenth century heralds as being exhibited in the church.

The fourteenth century font is slightly earlier than all this fifteenth century embellishment, but its quaint carvings of the Agnus Dei, St Peter in pontifical robes bearing a church, the resurrection of Christ, a chalice with wafer, the Baptism of Christ — St John holding a jug to pour the water — and the sacred monogram IHS all add to the decoration of the church. The carvings fill seven of the eight sides leaving a blank eighth side indicating that the font originally stood against a wall, rather than in its present position standing free under the tower arch. A possible medieval pun is contained in the carving of the Agnus Dei. The lamb is carved perfectly smooth, unlike the lamb on a similar font at Southfleet church a few miles away. The Southfleet lamb is very woolly, the Shorne lamb 'shorn'.

A profusion of lights and shrines glittered on every side of the church. In the north chancel, now filled by the vestry and organ, was the shrine of St Nicholas, and the altar of St John the Baptist. John Page before making his gift for the bell directed that he should be buried before 'the autrie of seynt John Baptist on the north side of the Church of Shorne'. A feature of this separate altar and shrine remains today in the fifteenth century oak screen dividing the north chancel from the main chancel, which was discovered practically intact in the 1870s when a lath and plaster wall which had long filled the arcade between the two chancels was pulled down.

On the south side of the chancel the old Randall chapel was by this time also known as the Lady chapel and contained the altar and shrine of 'our lady', to whose light pious John Page bequeathed a bushel of barley, whilst several other legacies to the same shrine or light show the veneration of the villagers to 'our lady'. Other lights to St James, St Erasmus, St Christopher, St Peter, St Anthony, and 'Our lady of pity' all maintained by gifts and legacies of the faithful glimmered around the church.

One last glimpse of the pre-reformation church is afforded in quite another context. A lease of the great tithes by the Dean and Chapter dated 1578 has survived in the Diocesan Archives, which contain a number of conditions referred to as being 'as of old time', no doubt following pre-reformation practice. It is indeed redolent of the middle ages. Among charges such as the ancient payment of ten shillings a year to the poor of Shorne, which survived until the twentieth century, there is a condition that the lessee supply 'green rushes to be strown in the Church of Shorne at the feast of Easter'. The rushes reflect an otherwise forgotten aspect of the church to set off the glitter of shrines and lights, painting and carving.

Now we pass from the church in its full flowering of the age with twinkling lights, rush-strewn floor, and graves with their new brasses beneath which rested some of those who have appeared in this story, and turn to the great changes of the sixteenth and seventeenth centuries.

1. Testamenta Cantiana Pg. 70

The old timber-framed Yeoman's Hall house now known as Little St Katherine's. When this photograph was taken it was used as three cottages, but it has now been restored to its original condition.

The Jacobean Communion table, purchased by the churchwardens in 1637 for £1.10.0. The extended ends on each side are later additions.

## Chapter 6
## THE DEVELOPMENT OF THE PARISH

Two generations after the rood screen had been so lovingly painted, the glow of faith had faded, and by the end of the sixteenth century the somewhat sparse history of Shorne founded on the church and the manor becomes the relatively well-recorded story of parochial affairs under the control of justices, vestry, churchwardens and overseers, about which we have quite copious information provided by parish and personal records.

The local details of the momentous religious changes of the sixteenth century are hidden from us. The dissolution of the monasteries was begun before the actual reformation by Bishop Fisher with his suppression of the Higham Nunnery, but the suppression of the Abbey of Bermondsey by Henry VIII, and the dissolution of Cobham Chantry by Lord Cobham, only changed the landlords and tithe owners to whom the villagers paid their rents and tithes — the tithes and rents went on as before. The Marian reaction, which witnessed the local flurries of the rebellion of Sir Thomas Wyatt with its somewhat comic battle of Rochester Bridge and bombardment of Cooling Castle, has a quieter and lovelier memorial at Shorne in the noble silver chalice bearing a hallmark of 1557 — perhaps the gift of some unknown local worthy to replace the sacred vessels dispersed during the previous decade. But the fading of the colour, and the substitution of Cranmer's liturgy for the 'mutter of the mass' are unrecorded.

For the local historian the most important event of those years was the injunction of Thomas Cromwell that all parishes were to keep registers of baptisms, marriages, and burials. This order was issued on the 5th September 1538, and the first entry in Shorne's registers is

1538   John Gyllvin was baptised ye XXII day of September " [1]

John Rosse, the vicar who complied so promptly with Cromwell's injunction, is also the first of many vicars to figure in the registers when in 1545 amongst the burials of that year appears the entry

July 21   John Rosse   Vicar here

So begins a sharpening of the focus of village history. Names such as 'Hermitage', still a village name, make their appearance, whilst 'William a labourer' 'John a Smyth' 'William a Thatcher' introduce the daily work of the villagers.

At the end of Elizabeth's reign came the poor law. The surviving almost continuous series of poor law accounts from 1598 until the 1830s, compiled by the churchwardens and overseers in books, large and small, are in some ways more important as a local record than the Registers. Their changing scripts, with their wildly fluctuating standard of orthography, the scratching and scribbling in the margins as the writer loosened up his quill before settling to work, the occasional pungent comment, all help to reflect not only poor relief, but the people amongst whom rates were collected and relief distributed. The history distilled from these accounts is expanded during the seventeenth and eighteenth centuries by scattered churchwardens' accounts, odd manor rolls, deeds and other personal documents, but the poor law accounts continuing decade after decade for over two centuries form a background linking other more sporadic resources at our disposal.

The accounts begin with an interesting little picture of how the poor law administration was introduced to the parish. The first Poor Law Act to apply generally to the country was passed in 1597, and in April 1598 Sir John Leveson and William Lambarde, two of the justices of the county, summoned the churchwardens of Shorne to attend upon them with four other local worthies, to be instructed in their new duties under the Act. Edward Armstrong and George Reignold — two local yeomen — were churchwardens that year, and they took with them two of the minor local gentry, George Page and Wigan Burstow, and two substantial yeomen, John Baynard and William Munn.

On entry into the magisterial presence, the six villagers were introduced to the new system and their duties. The magistrates promptly appointed all four of the uncommitted parishioners to be 'Collectors for the poor' (the title was later changed to 'Overseers') and delivered a lengthy 'charge' in nine articles defining their duties. The 'collectors' were to set down the names of the poor, assess the inhabitants, and apply the proceeds of such assessments in relief, placing apprentices, and building dwelling places for the poor. They were to account for any balance of cash in hand, license beggars, hold monthly meetings, and set down the names of those who defaulted in payment of the rates.

One may suspect that the parish officers were somewhat dazed by these quite peremptory instructions, and we may wonder at their comments as they rode homewards. They promptly purchased a quire of paper to set down the 'charges' before they forgot them, making a careful note to charge the 5d. the paper cost against the rate to be collected.

This episode introduces us to the churchwardens of the parish. Shorne is unfortunate in that it once had early pre-reformation churchwardens' accounts, which were purloined from the parish chest by Robert Pocock the Gravesend historian in about 1800, and which, after being mentioned by him and other antiquaries of that period, were lost when he was made bankrupt and sold up. We do however have a set of churchwardens' accounts covering the period between 1630 and 1680 which give us considerable information about the vestry, the parish officers, and parish administration in the seventeenth century.

At the Easter vestry the vicar presided over a mixed lot of vestrymen, who varied in their status from leading men of the village like the local squire, and substantial yeomen, to smallholders and local tradesmen. Judging from the signatures or marks on the accounts some two thirds of those attending were literate, to the extent of signing their names, but on the other hand the assembly seems to have been drawn from a limited number of families in the village, the same families cropping up in the lists generation after generation.

The first business of the vestry was to settle the accounts of the previous year, and with the coming of the poor law this involved two sets of accounts, one the church rate account, which was the concern of the churchwardens, and the other the poor law accounts which were checked by the vestry and then confirmed by the magistrates. Then the officers for the ensuing year were appointed; churchwardens, overseers, sidesmen, and three road surveyors (sometimes noted as for Shorne Street, Marshside and Thong respectively). The overseers' appointment had to be confirmed by the magistrates, but the rest were solely the affair of the vestry.

The accounts, particularly the churchwardens' accounts, reveal the surprisingly wide range of the duties of the parish officers. Many of the payments reflect ancient matters of medieval or even earlier origin. The church rate itself was an ancient charge on the landowners of the parish, of obscure origin, and though stated at the heading of each account to be for the repair of the roofs, walls and fences of the church, the precise way in which it was used helps us to follow something of village life in those days.

The first duty of every churchwarden on his election was to take the oath at the archdeacon's court and make his presentment, as he still does today. So the first entries in the church rate accounts are evocative; the leisurely jog to Rochester where he paid the Apparator a small fee (usually 4d.) for a book of articles, put in his presentment (another 4d.) and was duly sworn. When the formal part of the day was ended it was followed by a pleasing, but now long discontinued, practice. The churchwardens adjourned to a local inn, where they had a good dinner at the expense of the parish, the whole being recorded in entries such as

'Expended for the first visitation dinner and horsemeat and for swearing ye new churchwardens        12.6'

No doubt it was with a mellowed mind the churchwardens contemplated the troubles and chances of the year ahead, as they rode home.

The churchwardens' prime duty of maintaining the repair of the church will be more fully dealt with later, but year after year there are items for repairing the fences, the churchyard's stile, the gates, the roof, windows and bells.

The ringing of the bells was a constant small charge on the church rate. By custom the bells were rung on 5th November, King's coronation day, and King's birthday. For this the bellringers were regularly paid. The early entries say simply 'beer for the ringers', but by the end of the seventeenth century the payment had become fixed at 6s. 8d., or a noble, for each ringing, and by the middle of the nineteenth century when the church rate ceased, this payment was primly entered as 'a noble' without any reference to the bell ringers, though no doubt they still used the money for the original purpose of refreshment.

There were a number of regular payments from the church rate which seem to have little enough association with the church. Every half year a payment was made to the High Constable, of amounts between £1 and £2 'for gaol money and the house of correction'. Another amount regularly paid from the church rate to the High Constable was 'To the Bocton Blean Highway'. This payment of about £1 conceals under the curious name the identity of the Dover road passing through the parish. It seems to have been an ancient county charge, similar to the more irregular, but probably even more ancient, charge for the repair of county bridges, like the item in 1632 'paid to Teason (Teston) Bridge 13s. 4d.'.

Another obscure and ancient charge on the parish paid out of the church rate every year in the early seventeenth century was 'Lath Silver', 'Larkfield Head Silver' or some similar description, recording the payment of 3s. 4d. to the ancient lathe court. Probably the charge was associated with the ancient Kentish regality of Aylesford, the earlier name of the Lathe. The liability is one which Thomas Bishop tried to save the parish, when in 1527 he bequeathed to the churchwardens '40 moder sheep' from the produce of which the 'head money to the lathe of Lakefield' could be paid. By the seventeenth century the 'moder sheep' had long since gone leaving no trace, but this is but another example of the extensive spread of a churchwarden's duties.

Associated with these 'County' charges were the expenses of maintaining law and order. The village Borseholder (constable) was appointed by the manor court, but his expenses were paid by the churchwardens out of the church rate until the latter part of the seventeenth century when the payment tended to fall on the overseers and the poor rate. Hardly a year passes without the churchwardens paying the Borseholder for 'carrying a prisoner to gaol' or 'lodging of poor Irish'. The stocks and whipping post were also often repaired at the cost of the church rate.

Another charge was a primitive pest control. Year after year, between five shillings and twenty shillings was paid out of the church rate for heads of foxes and 'grays' (badgers) at a shilling a head. One wonders if the sportsman brought the gory trophy to the churchwarden's house during the week, or took it to church on Sunday. The idea was made into something of a sporting event in 1673 when two entries occur in the accounts.

'Paid more for 6 fox heads kild in the snow      6.0.
Expended at Widd. Terrys (she was a local alehouse
keeper) for bread and meat and beer at the fox hunting    12.0.'

For a brief moment we can see William Edward and William Jermin and their sporting friends stamping into the village inn out of the snow which held up all ploughing and field work, warming themselves with good cheer and a good fire after a hard day's hunting.

1. Another very important part of a churchwardens duties was the administration of the parish charity described in the next chapter.

## Chapter 7
## CHARITY AND THE POOR

There are traces of several charitable bequests for the benefit of the poor of the village from late medieval times, but apart from the 'parsonage money' paid by the Rectors of the parish already mentioned all seem to have disappeared by the seventeenth century. The gift of herrings by Thomas Davys was perhaps difficult to maintain: no doubt the vicar whose duty it was to distribute them was not very keen on the messy business. It seems hard to explain however how a definite charge of 6/8 per annum made by Thomas Bishop in favour of the poor on a house in Shorne Street disappeared. Thomas Pettit gave £10 'stock' which was to be lent out, the interest to be paid to the poor, and the churchwardens' accounts of the 1640s show how this became overlooked and forgotten during those troubled years.

At the end of the sixteenth century there was a not inconsiderable amount of casual charity to the village poor from the more wealthy who had interests in the village. Indeed these payments were so regular and important in village life that they were given the name 'Devocon money' and are usually listed separately in the early poor law accounts. For instance in 1602 the list reads:

| | |
|---|---:|
| 'More wh my Ld Grace of Canterbury gave | xxs. |
| More wh my Ld Cobham gave | xxs. |
| More wh ys given by the last will of Reignold Hawkes yearly | xxs. |
| More wh ys yearly given for Hutchynsensis gift | xs. |
| More wh ys yearly given by Mr Cheney of London ad bene . ... (?) | xxvjs. viijd.' |

These payments continue during the first decade of the seventeenth century but then disappear . . . We know why Lord Cobham's gift ceased — he was in the Tower — but the gift of the Archbishop (about which one would like to know more as he had no special association with the village) and the other 'yearly' bequests vanish, though Mr Cheney was to establish a more permanent charity by his will, as will be related later. At the time these bequests, with a total of over £4 a year, were of considerable importance in the life of the village poor, when the poor rate averaged only about £9 a year.

There are traces of old established custom about the payment of these amounts. Twice a year, at Easter and on St Thomas's day just before Christmas, the church bell was tolled, and the poor assembled at the church where the churchwardens distributed amounts of about 2s. to each applicant. Those receiving payment were not necessarily only those who were to be listed in the poor law accounts as 'poor and impotent people deserving of relief' but included others who were presumably on the fringes of poverty and thought worthy of some small help, particularly at Christmas, even though during the rest of the year they did not qualify for the new poor law payments.

During the early years of the seventeenth century these annual voluntary contributions were augmented, and then replaced, by the creation of more formal charitable trusts from which the village benefits even today.

The earliest was that of Lord Cobham (the father of the traitor lord) who, shortly before his death, put in hand the establishment of almshouses at Cobham on the site of the old college of chantry priests founded by his ancestor, and suppressed by his father. The almshouses were to provide places for villagers from all the villages in which Lord Cobham had estates, and as he was a large landowner in Shorne, being Lord of the Manors of Shorne, Randall, and Merston at his death, the village was allotted two places.

Lord Cobham's executors completed the establishment of the trust, which was placed in the hands of the Rochester Bridge Wardens as Trustees, and by 1600 the old college buildings were renovated. Two of Shorne's poor, Elizabeth Morrice, a blind widow, and Mother Carroll, who was lame, were accommodated in the picturesque old buildings behind Cobham Church. Both these old ladies were among those listed by the Shorne Overseers as poor and needing relief from the rates, and so from this early date we find the association of private charity with the poor law, which continued throughout the next two hundred years.

In 1618 the village received an important bequest under the will of Henry Adams of London. Henry Adams was a member of the Cutlers Company who from his will seems to have been a charitable man of a sociable disposition, with some idea of the dangers which beset a parish charity. He claims to have been born in Shorne, though his name does not appear in the early registers. There was indeed a family of Adams in the parish in the sixteenth century but the register of those early days does not appear to be entirely complete. The family were apparently ordinary village yeomen, with a poorer branch which we will meet in the Poor Law accounts, and Henry was obviously the village lad who had made his fortune in the City.

By his will he bequeathed to the village a rent charge of ten shillings to be paid to the man who each year collected the money for the parish, ten shillings a year to a godly preacher for a sermon on the anniversary of his death, and ten pounds per annum to be paid to the oldest and poorest of the parish at the discretion of the churchwardens and overseers, the payment to be made on the anniversary of his death each year.

This complicated bequest, supported by the self-interest of the churchwarden who collected the money, and the vicar who normally preached the sermon, was to survive all the vicissitudes of the following centuries. It also had an unplanned effect on parish custom. Mr Adams died on St Peter's day, 29th June. This was also the day of the church's patron saint, so the older distribution of alms at Easter time fell into abeyance and 29th June became an important day in the parish calendar when for the next two and a half centuries, the charity, soon to be known as 'Peter's Pence' in parish parlance, was distributed at the church door to the poorer villagers after they had dutifully listened to the 'Godly' sermon.

Seven years later in 1625 Richard Cheney, also of London, whose annual gift to the poor during his lifetime had formed part of the 'Devocon money', died, and by his will he bequeathed forty shillings a year to the parish to be paid to four poor men or women at the rate of two shillings and sixpence per quarter. The Cheneys were an old Kentish family and though their home was in East Kent they may have given their name to Cheneys Farm at Thong, but we know no more about Richard Cheney and his connection with the village. There were no special arrangements for the collection of this money, and though it survived until the present century, it was often uncollected for one reason or another. In contrast Henry Adam's special provisions saw that, if only from sheer self interest, the parish officers did their duty.

It was against this background of charity that the poor law was introduced to the village. The routine which was to be so important a part of parochial affairs for so long began with the return of the newly appointed overseers to the village in 1598.

In a previous chapter we have described the way in which they were appointed and instructed in their duties, but their handling of the business was much influenced by earlier village customs. For instance, though the magistrates had ordered that the rate was to be levied 'according to ability' 'without respect to those areas of land in their occupation' the older church rate had always been levied on an acreage basis, so the overseers simply levied a rate per acre over the whole parish, the amount per acre varying from year to year in accordance with the vestry's estimate of the probable amount which would be needed in the coming year. Likewise though the names of the poor are set out they are stated to be 'such as have already usually received relief from our poor box', ignoring the magistrates' directions as to the method of selecting suitable recipients of relief.

The lists of poor which they compiled for the first ten years or so of the poor law accounts were entered in detail at the beginning of each account, and were divided into three categories: the 'poor impotent folk', 'poor labouring folk . . . not able sufficiently by sickness or any other hyndrance . . . to help themselves' and the children 'fit to be apprenticed'. In the first list of 1598 there are eleven poor impotent folk, six able poor, and seven children fit for apprenticeship.

Of the poor 'impotent folk', there were five who were lame or aged fifty years or more, two simply 'unable to get' their living. Elizabeth Morrice was blind, but Mother Watcham, who was ninety years of age, was not considered necessarily to be relieved all the time her son at Cooling was able to help her. Two of the eleven are children: one 'Foxe of xiij years of age a lame boy going with stiltes living wholly on the alms of the parish' and John Adams a boy of eleven years 'so grievously tormented with the stone yt is not able to work but needs dayly relief'.

Of the other two lists most of the children 'fit for apprenticeship' seem to have been children of the labouring poor. For instance George Adams, an apprenticeable child of thirteen, was presumably a brother of the unfortunate John Adams, and one wonders if these Adams children were related to the generous and rich Henry Adams who had been a villager before he made his fortune in London.

Though listed, not all received any regular relief. The weekly amounts paid ranged from a shilling to only two or three pence and the payments are rarely for the whole of an uninterrupted year. In a time of winter hardship in February 1599 twenty-two individuals, some of whom do not appear in any of the lists of, as it were, official poor, received relief of a shilling or so. The older 'Devocon money' was also used to eke out the poor rate; for instance John Saunders received 6d. a week for the whole year 'besides a great pt of the money given upon devocon'.

The overseers also provided other relief. In 1604 there is a note in the accounts that they had built two tenements for old people on Shorne Hill, into which they had put 'old Mills and his wife' and an 'Old widow woman called Mother Hayles'. The sort of structure involved is indicated by the entry in the accounts showing that the two were built by a Thomas Brice for xlvjs. From later entries when the cottages were repaired it seems they were built of wattle and daub with a thatched roof. They continued to house paupers until the end of the eighteenth century, but the site of the cottages is now completely lost as the result of later gravel digging.

Illness was relieved as it arose. In 1601 George Adams was sick and was paid 6d. a week but finally was sent off to London 'to the hospital' at the cost of two shillings. 'Father Mills', in one of the parish tenements received similar small payments during his illness, and when he died leaving his widow in the cottage, the overseers gave her a special shilling 'since her husband died'.

A special case was that of Wigan Foxe the cripple lad 'going with styltes'. In the accounts from 1598 to 1602 there is a yearly note: 'Moreover we say we have allowed Wg Foxe going with styltes to begge by our appointment att certain houses therein lymited'.

His clothing was supplied by the parish. In 1599 he had 'Apparel' — a shirt and two pair of shoes — probably his disability wore out shoes rapidly and they were a necessity to him. Nothing however was paid to him in cash and he apparently subsisted on the casual charity of villagers by virtue of his begging licence.

By 1602 he was sixteen years of age and it seems that the village officers were stirred, perhaps by compassion. They approached the Darenth hospital and arranged for him to be housed there. They paid the hospital £6 (about half the total rate for that year) and provided him with new clothes:—

>  'More the apparrelling of Fox
>  for his shirt                         iijs.viijd.
>  For hose                                   xiid.
>  Cloth for jerkin and breeches         iijs.viijd.

One wonders how the youth settled at the 'Hospital or Almshouses at Darenth at Dartford'.

Besides the incidental notes about the poor themselves the accounts also give us glimpses of the villagers who were not 'poor and impotent' but who had their troubles. In each account there is a list of those who had not paid their rates. The first year of the rate is quite exceptional, for nine names are mentioned as 'behynd' in either the whole or part of the cess, and in spite of Edward Armstrong being a churchwarden (or perhaps because he was) we find the interesting note: 'John Armstrong was assessed at iis.vd. who after he hath manifested his poor estate we thought it good to spare him the cess'.

In 1601 Edward Armstrong himself (no longer churchwarden) is mentioned as 'Behynd for the whole assess'.

The outside world is also reflected in these early accounts. In 1606 a sum of twenty shillings was paid: 'For the relief of the poore of Cobham in the sickness time'.

Plague was reported in that year and Cobham College accounts refer to the plague in Cobham. Strangely enough Shorne seems to have escaped with only six deaths for all causes recorded in that year — rather less than the average.

Another outside charge on the rate was a species of County charge usually known as Gaole money. Whether it was the same charge as we find the churchwardens paying out of the church rate in the middle of the seventeenth century is not clear. The payment however was obviously not popular and apparently new when in 1600 the overseers record

>  It. to ye queens bench the 11th August         vis.vjd.
>  It. to ye Marshalsea even ye same time         xiijs.
>  It. to ye gaol and house of correction and
>     maimed soldiers                             xviijd.iiijd.

adding a note which speaks over the centuries for all tax payers: 'We pay this mony wholly to the constable and their acquittances can show how it is distributed we know not'.

We will return to the subject of the poor later in this history, but must now take up other events in the parish during the seventeenth century.

Shorne Street. This photograph was taken about 1962 looking north. The only remaining feature today is the iron railing on the roadside.

A view of Shorne village in c.1953, from what is now Warren View. Note the old mill on centre sky line.

## Chapter 8
## THE CIVIL WAR AND SHORNE

The churchwardens' accounts for 1631 record a payment for the ringing of the bells 'when the king visited Rochester and the Bishop came to Shorne' and another 'for oates when the King was at Rochester'. King Charles was inspecting his ships at Chatham, and was met at Shorne by the Bishop of Rochester on the borders of the Bishop's ancient 'Liberty'. The royal cavalcade probably halted for a few minutes on the dusty Dover Road somewhere near the Crown Halfway House, whilst the royal and episcopal parties exchanged courtesies, and the villagers had the opportunity of paying their loyal duty to their sovereign. Whilst the villagers gazed respectfully at the thin haughty face of their king, he, no doubt, looked with bored condescension on what was to him a common enough sight in his travels, a group of villagers headed by the local gentry in their homespun finery, supported by yeomen and tradesmen in respectable sober attire, with a fringe of village labourers, a few women and a scatter of children, all against a background of fields, trees and hedges in their spring finery, with the sound of bells in the distance.

After the royal party had moved off, William Armstrong the churchwarden (probably the son of Edward Armstrong the churchwarden of 1598) trudged off up the rutted village road to the church where he paid the bellringers for their trouble (and their beer) before returning to his home at Thong. Probably neither he nor his fellow villagers realised that this colourful incident was a prelude to some thirty years of change and stress in the nation, which would have its side effects on the quiet life of the village.

The decade which followed, one in which national discontent with the royal policy in church and state grew, passed quietly enough in Shorne. Probably at this time the altar table stood in the body of the church, but Richard Balam the vicar was no puritan. He wore a surplice for which the churchwardens paid an annual sum of one shilling for 'washing the surplice'. Mr Balam had been vicar since 1629, and was also the vicar of Cobham. Before his appointment he had been the headmaster of King's School Rochester. In spite of his Cobham living he resided at Shorne, at first at the old vicarage, then called the 'Cross House', but later he acquired a house on Shorne Ridgeway where, according to an old manor roll, he had a messuage and about four acres of land at a quit rent of 20d.

In 1634 Laud was appointed Archbishop of Canterbury and instituted a series of visitations throughout the country seeking out what might be amiss in parochial religious observance. There is an entry in the churchwardens' accounts in 1634 'For the metropolitical visitation dinner' which is followed by one or two items suggesting only minor shortcomings from the Laudian point of view.

A new surplice was purchased for thirty shillings, but the churchwardens prudently sold the old surplice for a few pence.

More changes came in the following year. In 1636 the Archbishop ordered all communion tables to be railed off at the east end of the church, and Shorne quickly complied. The entries in the accounts tell the tale:—

| | |
|---|---|
| 'For deales for the communion rail | 1. 9. 0. |
| For carriage | 3. 3. |
| Paid William Singleton for work about the rails | 2. 2. 0. |
| Paid John Pettit for ironwork | 5. 4. |

The total amount spent was a substantial proportion of the church rate and the promptness of compliance with the Laudian directive suggests that the majority of the village led by the vicar accepted the 'Beauty of holiness' upon which the archbishop set such store.

The activities of the next three or four years support this idea. In 1637 when Gervayse Maplesden the tanner was churchwarden the parish was quite heavily rated for church rate at 1d. per acre for the first half year and 2d. per acre for the second half year, and a considerable amount of work was done in and about the church. Probably the force behind this work was an archidiaconal visitation in that year, for a dinner is noted 'when he visited the church'.

Probably the new altar rails made the old altar table look shabby, for it had had to be repaired in 1631, and moving it to the eastern end of the chancel had not improved matters. So in 1637 a new communion table was purchased for £1.10.0d, William Cottrel carting it to the village. It almost certainly survives as the altar table in the Randall Chapel today, and possibly the old table now in the north aisle is the earlier one. To improve the general appearance of the sanctuary mats were purchased to put about the new table, whilst wainscoting is mentioned as being put up. Before the restoration in the 1870s the whole of the east wall of the sanctuary and the lower part of the east window was covered by a large and not particularly attractive reredos which provided a somewhat clumsy backing to the altar.

A considerable amount of other carpentry is indicated by the entries in the churchwardens' accounts for this and the following years. Details are not given but there seem to have been some new pews in the nave, and a three decker pulpit was built. A new prayer book costing 6d. and a Book of Homilies costing 6s.0d. were purchased for the new desk.

Some of the details given are of casual interest: for instance John Baynard was paid 'for a timber bat'. Material seems to have come from London by water, there being entries for carriage and wharfage, 'for boat hire to and fro' 'for bringing the stuff from London' for 'fetching it from Gravesend' which suggests that the 'stuff' came from London on the tide boats to Gravesend and was then carted to Shorne, the waggoners getting 4d. 'for drink'.

The roof was also giving trouble. Old William Armstrong had done much work to the wooden shingles which covered the nave some years before, and further work had to be done in 1640. The lead on the south aisle roof was also defective, the plumber being paid a sizeable bill of £3.15.6d. 'for lead and works and other things'. A dial and post were also provided. A final touch inside the church was a carpet costing £2.13.5d. purchased for the communion table.

In 1640, however, came the first sign of the stir in the world around. The summonsing of the Short and Long parliaments were each accompanied by the ordering of a nationwide solemn fast for the success of parliamentary deliberations, and these are recorded in the Shorne accounts by two entries 'for two books for the fast' and later 'for the book for the last fast'.

Naturally the quarrels and differences of King and Parliament are not reflected in the parish records, but in 1642 the Irish rebellion raised in its most acute form the question of whether King or Parliament should control the army. The rebellion must have been common knowledge in Shorne, because in 1642 the Dover Road seems to have been thronged with Irish refugees. A shilling was given to 'a poor Irish protestant undone by the rebels there'. A 'poor Irish woman great with child' received 2s.0d. — no doubt to get her out of the parish quickly. Again in June a 'poor traveller coming out of Ireland' received a shilling and in July '4 more poor travvelers that had lost all in Ireland' were relieved with two shillings.

The first impact of parliamentary rule came before the end of the fateful year 1642, not by troops or war, but by parliament's early exercise of the power which, as much as Cromwell's genius, was to make it victorious — the power of the purse. Each county under parliamentary control was levied, and before the end of the year John Clay and William Webb the churchwardens were disturbed to receive a demand through the county committee that parishes were to assess the local contribution to this levy.

Mr Richard Parker, a local magistrate living at Pipes Place, lent the services of his clerk, and the vestry then met three or four times at Widow Bellingham's inn, to settle what was to be done, finally recording the episode in the terse entries:—

> 'Paid to Mr Parker's clerk for writing and
> perfecting of 4 certificates for our parish
> of the £400,000                                        10. 0.
> Item to the Widd. Bellingham for our expenses
> at three or four meetings about the said cess.    5. 0.

In the middle of 1643 vicars and churchwardens were required to subscribe to the 'Oath and Covenant', and William Webb the churchwarden purchased for a shilling 'a register for the oath and covenant'. The remainder of the year however seems to have been uneventful. Bread and wine for Palm Sunday and Easter Day were purchased as usual, the church linen washed, and some twenty-four more 'poor Irish' relieved. There must, however, have been some tension, perhaps connected with the willingness or otherwise of the vicar and churchwardens to subscribe to the 'Oath and covenant', for in 1644 the churchwarden's accounts record two significant entries.

> 'Item laid out when the minister and
> churchwardens were warned in before
> the Comitee                                            3. 2.

then a few lines later comes the item:

> 'Paid John Webbe for billeting of souldiers by
> the hand of Richard Parker                             8. 4.

The result of the summons is clearly that the Rev. Balam was suspended from his living. He no longer signs the accounts, and for two or three years seems to have been absent from the village, and when he returned he no longer lived in the old vicarage, but in his house on the Ridgeway taking no part in either church or parish affairs.

The actions of a troop of puritan soldiers in the village may be associated with a bill of £1.5.0d. to the glazier – Shorne has no ancient glass – and there is an ancient village tradition that 'Cromwell's men' destroyed the old rood screen. It had certainly disappeared by the eighteenth century and the puritans are as good a scapegoat as any.

1644 was the last year of the old order, and for several years the churchwardens' accounts are confused, whilst the parish registers end their regular recording of baptisms and deaths. The accounts for 1644 were approved by a vestry, from which Mr Balam was absent, in February 1645, but no assessment was made for church rate, no officers appointed, and Edward Armstrong, one of the churchwardens of 1644, seems to have carried on without formal appointment, and without a colleague. His accounts for 1645 are sparse and cover the period from 1645 to June 1646. They are markedly puritan in tone. Bread and wine were purchased for festivals, identified by date only. Thus the 22nd March was probably Palm Sunday, and the 29th March, Easter Day.

The next recorded vestry was held in August 1646 and the entries mark yet more change. In the first place the Rev. Balam is replaced by a 'Minister', Thomas Southall; and secondly the vestry seems to have been well attended, but not by the usual vestrymen. Of the seven names appearing, only John Clay and Edward Armstrong represent the former vestry, whilst Richard Parker, Thomas Miller, John Penny, Thomas Taylor, and Chas. Brigson made their first appearance as vestrymen. Thomas Carter and Edward Armstrong were appointed churchwardens 'according to a former election' which may have been at the meeting in February 1645 when the assessment was made. Richard Parker was of course the squire at Pipes Place, but none of the newcomers were poor, the smallest acreage for which they were rated being thirty acres, and three of them were assessed for over a hundred acres. Some were to hold office of one sort or another throughout the period to 1658, but are less conspicuous afterwards. We may perhaps assume that they represented the hardcore puritan element in the parish.

No church rate appears to have been either assessed or collected for the years 1646 and 1647, nor are there any recorded payments for the maintenance of the church or even the routine payments to the County. The next record is in April 1648 when a list of officers chosen is noted. John Clay and Rejoice Head were churchwardens, James Staines and Thomas Miller collectors for the poor, with Henry Parker, Hugh Collier and Richard Peck as surveyors. No vicar or minister is listed as having been at the vestry. The absence of a minister is explained by Walker's Suffering of the Clergy, which records that Thomas Southwell (whom Walker does not seem to have realised was an intruded puritan minister) was so neglectful of his parish of Shorne, that he was summonsed before the County Committee and suspended in 1648/9.

The April 1648 note of the appointment of officers is followed by another note dated March 1649[1], which records the appointment of new officers, and notes an assessment as 'made in Midsummer last past'. Again no 'Minister' is named as having been present.

The assessment was apparently collected with difficulty and was audited in July 1649 at a vestry when a new 'Minister' was present in the person of George Bladworth, who signed the accounts as 'Minister' followed by the signatures of the two churchwardens appointed in March 1649. Of the rates assessed the accounts show that only about two thirds were collected. It is worth noting that this was the time when the war came closest to the village when to suppress the Kentish rising the parliamentary army under Fairfax marched through the neighbouring village of Meopham. One would like to suppose that perhaps a third of the villagers joined the royalists and therefore could not pay their rate. On the other hand it must be remembered that that year the weather was notoriously bad, with incessant rain and poor harvests, so the reason for the non-payment of rates may well have been poverty alone.

George Bladworth (or Bludworth — the spelling varies) seems to have held the sinecure living of Merston since 1642, which may account for his appearance at Shorne, but he also seems to have held, probably as lessee, the Rectorial tithes of Shorne, and he continued to be rated for these tithes for a short while after he left the parish. He was still minister when the accounts of 1649 (including an assessment made in January 1649) were followed for the first time for some years in proper sequence on 15th April 1650 by a vestry when as 'Minister' assisted by eight vestrymen he signed the accounts. The vestry then appointed new officers, the record being approved under seal a few days later by Peter Buck and Charles Bowles, Magistrates.

The two new churchwardens, Henry Parker and Jarvis Maplesden, are worth a passing note. Henry Parker was the son of Richard Parker from Pipes Place who had died in 1646. Henry Parker continued to reside at Pipes Place and became a prominent figure in parish affairs during the rest of his life. His family was probably of the parliamentary connection. Richard Parker had been subseneschal of Gravesend when the Duke of Richmond was High Steward of the town. On the Duke being named as a Malignant, the Corporation of Gravesend had a change of heart and offered the High Stewardship to Oliver Cromwell who commissioned John Parker his understeward. John Parker seems to have been the brother of

The Post Office. An old post card showing the building before its red brick was covered with plaster. The brick conceals an older timber-framed building.

Henry, and when the Corporation of Gravesend went royalist again at the Restoration, they promptly ejected John Parker from his under-stewardship. Henry Parker, however, was a good middle-of-the-road man. Between 1649 and 1652 he was continuously churchwarden of Shorne with the approval of the County justices, though after this he was content to let Staines, Masters and the other puritans take the parish offices. He attended vestry meetings throughout the interregnum, and after the Restoration he continued to attend vestries, holding parochial office from time to time.

Jarvis Maplesden also regularly attended vestry meetings during this period and later. His family will be fully considered later – it was part of Shorne history for a century and a half – but at this point it is only necessary to remark that this Jarvis was the son of Jarvis Maplesden who had been a tanner at Little Moor on the Ridgeway from the beginning of the century. Old Jarvis had died in 1645 leaving his son to take over the business. The growing wealth of the family will be dealt with more fully later, but at this point it is proper to note that Jarvis the second received a commission as a captain in the militia raised by parliament. His company was ordered to join Cromwell for the battle of Worcester, but did not arrive in time – and from time to time in the later accounts he is referred to as Captain Maplesden. Like his father and like Henry Parker he attended vestries constantly throughout his life.

Year by year these two men attended vestries, usually heading the list of names or signatures, and there is little doubt that it was to these two men that we should attribute the ending of the period of confusion in parish affairs which followed the suspension of the Rev. Balam.

This confusion was not confined to churchwardens' accounts. The Parish Registers, those orderly records of the three fundamentals of society, become quite chaotic during the period. Volume one of the registers (the fair copy on vellum made at the beginning of the seventeenth century) had become more or less filled before the civil war began. The marriage section ended in 1630, burials in 1641, both for lack of space, but the section for baptisms had still a page or so to fill. There is a note in the churchwardens' accounts in the early 1630s of the purchase of another register book, but this book is lost. The baptismal entries however continue on a regular basis until the suspension of the Rev. Balam, after which there are a number of entries in his handwriting, by no means consecutive, which suggest that on his suspension he kept the old register, leaving the new one for the Rev. Southall or one of his successors to lose or destroy. That the missing book was still available for a time is suggested by the fact that that new register established by parliamentary ordinance, which now forms the second volume of the parish registers, begins with some entries earlier in date than the beginning of this new official book, with a note '1648/9 no register kept'. It is also clear that when the Rev. Balam returned to the village some of the villagers took advantage of his presence for unofficial baptisms, with entries in the old register all in the Rev. Balam's handwriting.

The new register ordered by the government was at first in the hands of civilian 'Registers', two of whom were appointed in quick succession for Shorne, William Minto in 1654 and John Starling in 1655. Neither seems to have been a local man. An examination of the names of those registered by Mr Balam and by the 'Registers' suggests that several villagers played it safe. For instance John Clay, who had been churchwarden in the period of confusion, had the births of a son and daughter entered by Mr Balam in the old register, and then when the new register was officially opened, had the baptisms of five other children between 1646 and 1654 entered at the beginning of the new book.

Even though the beginning of the 1650s indicates some return to the older regular vestries, matters did not go smoothly for the next two or three years. The accounts for 1650 were not approved until much later and the next assessment is in May 1652, whilst the next recorded list of officers chosen by the vestry appears to be dated 12th March 1653. The accounts for 1650 have one or two items which may have some hidden significance. In 1650 six soldiers were billeted in the village with orders for quarters, though they could not have stayed long as the amount involved is only 2s.5d. The entry is followed in the accounts by two payments for 'fixing ye glass in ye church', the second being for the substantial sum of £3.5.0d. Then the stocks were repaired and new handcuffs bought, indicating the firmer enforcement of law and order. Finally there is another item:

> 'Paid Kitchingham for plastering ye font
> with lime and haire          2. 6.'

The medieval carvings on the font may have given offence to the puritans, and we must be grateful that the churchwardens thus saved the ancient font, rather than smashing it, or throwing it into the nearest pond.

During this period another change took place which suggests that the Rev. Bladworth was no better than the Rev. Southall. He did not sign the 1650 accounts, which were approved in April 1653 and when an assessment was raised in October 1653 the list of vestrymen is headed by one John Stacey 'clerk'. In later accounts he corrects this to 'Minister'.[2] Under his leadership the routine of vestry administration seems to have revived. During 1653 the churchwardens purchased a 'frame for ye basin' – no doubt the basin replaced the popish font; and also a 'Velvet cushion for the pulpit' costing £3.13.4d., which suggests that the new minister was a great believer in the puritan sermon.

During 1654 we can infer from the accounts that civil government was being sorted out. For instance the old payment of Lathe silver to the High Sheriff had fallen well into arrears during the troubled years, but during this year the authorities required payment of all arrears and after some delay some eight years' arrears were paid. Another step taken by the Cromwellian government was the regularising of the system for repair of roads. In 1654 the old corvée road mending was replaced by a road rate, which continued until the Restoration, and as a result we have a road rate book for this period, from which it is possible to follow the system of hiring farmers' carts and employing casual labour to keep the roads in some sort of order.

A typically puritan item occurs in the accounts when Henry Cugley was fined £1 for 'selling drink unlicensed' and William Mumford 10s.0d. for 'selling drink on a fast day'. This was in 1653, and in the following year all the alehouse-keepers were fined a collective twenty shillings for 'selling of drink on ye Sabbath day'.

John Stacey last appears in the accounts in 1654 and in the following year the accounts are signed by John Barnes 'Minister'. Under his chairmanship the annual vestries met regularly, but the annual church rate dropped to four or five pounds a year, this including payments to the Constable of 'gaole money' amounting to £2.2.8d. a year, leaving little enough to spend on the neglected church. Suggestive of the outlook of those days is the fact that in 1657 the local blacksmith Thomas Williams was paid two shillings out of this small rate for 'a payer of iron handcuffs for the whiping post'.

In 1657 John Barnes died, apparently somewhat suddenly, for there is a single note in the Poor Law accounts in that year:—

> 'Paid to poore people having a breife to
> bee read our minister Mr Barnes being
> dead I sent them away with          2. 0.'

and 'John Barnes' without the usual reference to his clerical status is briefly noted as having been buried at Shorne on the 30th August.

Perhaps the times were already changing. No new minister seems to have been appointed. In April 1658 the churchwardens' meagre accounts were audited by the vestry and new officers appointed without the presence of a 'Minister', 'Vicar' or 'Clerk'. In that year the Protector died and perhaps there was no urgency for a new minister. No doubt Mr Balam who was still living quietly on Shorne Ridgeway, paying his church rate of a few pence, was able to fulfil unofficially any requirements of his old office. 1659 passed with orderly vestries, without incident, and without a minister.

Then in 1660 came the news that the King was returning and would indeed pass through Shorne on his way to London. No doubt the villagers watched the King that early May morning, as they had watched his father thirty years before. Then they returned to settling their own affairs.

In the accounts of 1659/60 is the significant entry

  'For setting up the Kings arms      £1. 10. 0.'

and the spirit of the Restoration is still proudly displayed in the church today where the royal arms so set up (a solid piece of carving bright with gilding and paint) still displays the royal motto as

'Dieu est mon droit'

a subtle comment on village loyalty through those trying years. Which of the village royalists allowed himself this last thrust when he presented the arms?

So with a glance at our old altar purchased in 1637 and the royal arms to remind us of village reactions to this troubled period, we turn to an aftermath of purely parochial affairs, little touched by outside politics.

1. If the end of the year was March, as was customary in those days, this suggests a break of nearly two years between meetings.
2. There was at this time a John Stacey vicar of Ridley near Meopham (1649 to 1680). Though the puritans objected to a clergyman holding more than one living it seems possible that John Stacey of Ridley was the 'minister' at Shorne.

Crown Lane, looking west, before modern housing construction, as seen from the green in front of the Post Office.

The view from Crown Lane before post war building. Pipes Place is in the middle distance to the right of the scene and St Katherine's in the centre.

## Chapter 9
## RESTORATION AND STABILITY

During the two decades following the Restoration the parish settled into a rhythm which continued for over a century. The churchwardens resumed their pre-revolutionary routine, Visitations, bells for coronation day and the 5th November, bread and wine for church festivals, all as of old time. In 1662 the new prayer book was purchased for 7s.6d. and a new surplice for £2.10.0d. A prayer book for the clerk was also bought at the lower price of 2s.4d. The following year 'Flagons and a cloth for the communion table' were purchased. All this was no doubt the result of increased activity in the restored diocese. In 1661 Nicholas Loft, the churchwarden, notes the payment of six shillings 'paid to the sumner for warning me into Rochester six several times'. Richard Balam continued to preside at vestries each year, but he was an old man and his signature on the vestry accounts becomes noticeably shaky.

Yet little enough seems to have been done to the church during those years. From time to time one or other of the village craftsmen was paid a small sum for 'work about the church' which looks like patchwork. Probably Mr Balam, who had seen so many changes, was not keen to press for any work which would need a large church rate which might offend the puritan element.

Mr Balam's last attendance at the vestry was in April 1669. Shortly afterwards he resigned the living, a Mr Charles Bowles being inducted into the living in his place. Mr Bowles signed the accounts which were audited in December 1670, but the registers then conclude the story of both the old and the new vicar. The burial of Richard Balam 'late vicar of this parish' is recorded on the 21st November 1670, and that of Charles Bowles 'late vicar of this parish' on the 16th December the same year.

Mr Bowles' successor was Thomas Ayerst, who only a couple of years or so after coming to the parish married Elizabeth Maplesden and thus founded a line which was to prosper and have long associations with the village. His appointment to the living was the signal for a start to be made in repairing the church, and the steps taken and the work done can be followed in the churchwardens' accounts. They make an interesting picture of seventeenth century methods.

In 1671 after the churchwardens' visitation at Rochester (when 15s.6d. was spent on their dinner and horsemeat) came an archidiaconal visit to the parish itself:

> 'May 10 Paid to the chancellor and Mr Stowell
> when they came for to visit the church and
> vicarage house for dinner                £1. 8. 2.'

The next two years seem to have been occupied with negotiation, and perhaps evasion, occasioning more attendances before Mr Stowell. In April 1674 a church rate of the unprecedented amount of two shillings in the pound was agreed by the vestry, and collected, after the churchwardens had been again summoned 'concerning the repair of the church'. Then in August 1675 another assessment of two shillings in the pound was levied, and during the following year a vast amount of repair work was done to the church.

The principal trouble was the roof and the Randall Chapel. The ancient shingles on the nave roof and the lead flats on the south aisle and the north chancel were leaking, and the woodwork beneath the leads was rotten. The chapel was quite ruinous.

The opening moves are evocative. Luddesdown church had just undergone some repairs which had necessitated the use of a specially long ladder and scaffolding belonging to Cobham Hall, and an entry brings the picture before us:

> 'Paid for bringing the great ladder and two
> poles from Luddesdown church and one
> pole from Cobham Hall                    5. 6.'

Material was acquired from all quarters. Thomas Lease the village blacksmith supplied 4d. and 10d. nails in hundreds. Four thousand bricks and some lime was purchased from one John Shaw and eight loads of lime from Charles Hunt. Fourteen loads of chalk were dug and carted at the cost of £1.6.0d. and 13,400 tiles were acquired for the substantial sum of £15.15.6d.

The repair of the Randall chapel seems to have had first priority and Thomas Wellard and James Warren, two local craftsmen, were mainly responsible. Thomas Wellard had to make two journeys to Maidstone in connection with this work, and the churchwardens hired a mare from John Stone and a horse from Widow Armstrong to enable him to make the journeys as well as paying his expenses. The actual work on the chapel was the only fixed price contract job, a figure of £50 being agreed with the churchwardens. It seems the chapel was practically rebuilt. The east wall was rebuilt in brick, and the whole of the walls around it raised by some two feet. The timbers of the roof were renewed and the old shingles from the old roof sorted, the good ones being used to renew the roof of the nave, while the new roof of the chapel was tiled.

The replacement of the defective lead on the south aisle and the north chancel proved inexpensive. The old lead with its higher silver content was collected and sent off to Rochester where it was exchanged for a quantity of lead sufficient to replace the old at no charge except the cost of carting. One entry is sufficient to illustrate what went on:

> 'Paid to William Ward for the carriage of
> 63 hundred and a quarter of a 100 and
> 14 lb of old lead to Rochester and
> bringing from Rochester 62 hundred one
> half hundred and 19 lb of new lead and 80
> deal boards                              £1. 9. 6d.'

Inside the church it seems that the somewhat unusual ceiling of the nave was already in position, there being a number of entries about laths for the roof over the body of the church and many bushels of hair for the plaster work. The occasion for this plaster work ceiling was probably when the church was first roofed with shingles. There are indications on the tower that the original roof line was some nine inches to a foot higher than the present roof which indicates a thatched roof. The underside of thatch could be made sightly with whitewash, and thatch was draught proof. Shingles were not only draughty but their underside was quite unsightly. It was easier and cheaper to put the present ceiling across the nave than to remove and reline the shingle roof. The small doorway into the nave roof, off the flat roof of the south aisle, was 'made up' at the cost of six shillings. Probably this was the occasion when the small wrought iron crescent moon was fixed to this door, where it still serves the superstition which led to its being so fixed.

Most of the work was done by direct labour. The carpenters, plasterers, bricklayers and plumbers were all paid by the day. For instance Thomas Wellard after he had finished the Randall Chapel roof did much other work recorded by items such as:—

> 'For 6 days and a half for himself and
> 7 days his boy in repairing the roof under
> the lead on the south side of the church    £2. 13. 4.'

The plumbers working on the lead roof were supplied with

> 'A bushel and a half of coal to heat the plumbers iron'

Casual items remind us of the labour needed to supply even the most elementary needs:

> 'Paid to the Widow Armstrong for
> carrying water to the bricklayers    1. 2d.'

One can visualise the old lady jogging to and fro from the village pump in the Street (or perhaps from the pond behind the churchyard) with her yoke and buckets.

All the work was urged merrily on by items like

> 'Paid for beer for the plumbers,
> carpenters and bricklayers    14. 0d.'

By the end of 1676 the interior of the church was whitewashed and the whole work completed. Mr William Jermin, the churchwarden who seems to have supervised the whole of the work, sent back to Cobham Hall the 'great ladder' and marked the end of the work by the payment of 5s.0d. 'For ladders and pailes broken' and another 3s.0d. 'to my boy for work about the church'.

During the time the work was being done William Jermin was not only engaged on church repairs. Apart from the usual duties of a churchwarden, relieving wayfarers and paying the odd shilling for fox-heads, he had to sort out the charities which he and his colleagues were supposed to administer. It seems that during the 1670s the vestry had realised that the charities so worthily set up in pre-commonwealth days had been neglected.

One charity indeed disappears during this period. A sum of £10 had been bequeathed to the parish for the churchwardens to lend out to deserving cases at interest, the interest to be paid to the poor. It was always troublesome and there are indications even before the Civil war that lending the money and collecting the interest often caused the churchwardens trouble, and on at least two occasions legal action had had to be taken to recover the money. In 1650 the money had been lent to James Staines. In 1652 James Staines is recorded as a churchwarden and interest was paid on the £10 that year. After that the item fades from the accounts.

However, encouraged no doubt by Mr Ayerst, the churchwardens decided to look into the charities. Whereas the Adams Charity, because of the detailed arrangements made for its collection, was being regularly received and distributed, the Cheney charity had fallen away. The vestry indeed seems to have been uncertain of its rights under this bequest and obtained a copy of Mr Cheney's will. The churchwardens of St Mary Woolnoth were supposed to pay the annual sum of two pounds to Shorne out of moneys and lands bestowed on them by Mr Cheney, but Shorne had had nothing for years. After some negotiation Mr Jermin succeeded in obtaining the sum of £10 or five years arrears, though whether this was the true arrears is not clear; probably no one was sure. Mr Jermin was allowed one pound out of the total for his trouble in getting the money and the remainder was distributed among the poor in one distribution.

There was another matter which the vestry decided to look into. There was a rumour that Lady Eleanor Page (the widow of Sir William Page whose memorial she had erected in the church before her death) had in her will given something for the benefit of the parish, but the details were unknown to the vestry. Lady Page had died in 1645 and so the vestry obtained a copy of her will. This presented problems. In her will she had given fifty pounds to her executor Mr John Parker to buy a piece of land to be vested in four or more substantial freeholders of the parish, the yearly rents from such land to be employed in the payment of premiums for the apprenticeship of poor children of the parish, the children to be chosen by the churchwardens and overseers. She had further directed that the land should be purchased within two years of her death and her will ends with a prayer that 'neither my intention be frustrated nor the poor defrauded'.

The churchwardens then sought out the former Cromwellian sub-seneschal of Gravesend (whom one suspects had fallen on ill times with the Restoration) enquiring the whereabouts of the land purchased and what rents were in hand. The enquiry was delicate since John Parker was a brother (or other relation) to Henry Parker of Pipes Place, the leader of the vestry, and no doubt the enquiry was made through Henry Parker.

What followed is suggestive. On the 7th November 1675 the churchwardens noted in their book

'Forty shillings being the last years rent of the land purchased with part of Lady Pages gift to the poor of Shorne was then distributed among them'.

Nothing is said about the arrears, and the money was distributed among the poor in spite of the clear directions in Lady Page's will, which the churchwardens had carefully copied into their account book. In fact no land had been purchased by John Parker. This is confirmed two years later when the churchwardens note the receipt of forty shillings simply as 'interest'. It seems that the vestry realised that John Parker had appropriated the legacy for his own use, and were content to connive at this breach of trust by simply taking 'interest' year by year, and compounded their negligence by distributing the money amongst the poor without the slightest attempt to put poor children out as apprentices.

No doubt under the leadership of Henry Parker the vestry were diffident about taking any strong line with John Parker, the family of Parker constituting too powerful an influence with their local squirearchy and legal connections for simple vestrymen to tackle.

The matter was remedied to some extent when John Parker died in 1683. Pressure on his estate produced the sum of £45, which the vestry promptly caused to be invested in the purchase from a Mr Etkins of a piece of land described as being at Gads Hill, which for many years afterwards was known as the Parish field. The land was vested in four trustees; Henry Parker, William Woodyear (Lord of the manor of Shorne), William Cottmar and Jarvis Maplesden. The total legacy of £50 was never recovered and everyone seems to have been content to let this somewhat reduced and long delayed fulfilment of Lady Page's wishes settle the matter. We shall return to the vicissitudes of this charity later.

An old photograph of the original See Ho before it was burnt down in the 19th century. The name was formerly So Ho, an old hunting cry. Records of the inn go back to the 17th century.

The modern See Ho, showing the open situation before recent rebuilding. The land in the foreground was the local allotments.

## Chapter 10
## THE DOVER ROAD, INNS AND TANNERIES

For many centuries the most important road in Shorne was the Dover Road, which spanned the parish from Deadman's Bottom on the boundaries of Chalk in the west to the wooded crest of Gads Hill at Shorne's eastern boundary with Higham parish. Until the coming of the railway, this road was the main artery along which passed the traffic of the country between London and the Continent. Until the road was turnpiked in 1711 the parish had paid a regular county rate for the maintenance of the 'Bocton Blean Highway'.

The passing pageantry of the rich, and even occasional royalty, provided colour to a community life normally dully domestic. Though there were seldom occasions like the visit of the Emperor Charles V to Henry VIII in 1522 when it is said his retinue numbered 2,000 persons, we have already noted the ceremonial of the passing of Charles I on his way to inspect his ships at Chatham, and no nobleman could be expected to travel without a considerable entourage. But the great leave little mark on our records, whilst at the other extreme our parish books contain numerous records of the continuous flow of the poor vagrants travelling on their occasions along the Dover Road.

A careful churchwarden can suddenly bring the highway to life. In 1631, for instance, 'a scottish gentleman who beg'd with a license' received two shillings and six pence, whilst a 'poor scollar' received two shillings. In the following year 'Egyptians' were given two shillings and six pence to get them out of the parish. All nationalities passed along the highway. The Irish (who have already appeared in this history after the Irish Rebellion of 1642) were the most frequently relieved, but a Welsh woman is mentioned in 1657, whilst Scots, gentlemen or otherwise, were relieved on many occasions. Probably the most exotic passengers were 'three Turks' in 1721, but Frenchmen are mentioned more than once, beginning with 'A poor frenchman who was found dead at Gads Hill' in 1621 and buried in the churchyard. Passing seamen, shipwrecked or simply making their way from port to port were frequently at the churchwardens' door. 1675 was a bad year for seamen. There is the somewhat unusual item 'Eleven poor seamen redeemed from Argious' who only got a shilling between them. 'Seven seamen who lost their ship coming from Barbadoes' and 'Richard Griffin and four other seamen travelling out of Cornwall to Hartlepool' are all entries in the same year. The last party seems to have been well off course on land, but the churchwarden William Jermin, whose geography was perhaps equally as shaky, enters the item without comment.

Sometimes the entries read like the plot of a novelette, as on the occasion recorded by the Rev. Caleb Parfect in 1764 when, after the entry of the burial of 'Joseph Robinson a stranger' he goes on

'The mother of the child on my enquiring after the nature of his death etc and if he had ever been baptised produced a certificate of wh the following is a copy "This is to certify that Joseph the son of Edward and Margaret Robinson was baptised the 21st June 1764 by me John Haywood dissenting minister of Potters Bury in the County of Northamptonshire chaplain to the right honorable Earl Temple". The mother own'd she had been very wild that her father was a dissenting minister in Scotland, liv'd in great reputation and that she had been a disgrace to the family by eloping with a soldier etc. By the certificate it seems as if the soldier and the woman were at last married, though she gave a very blind account of her husband and was herself returning to Scotland'.

If we would add to the melodrama we may spare a thought for the woman trudging all the way from Potters Bury to Shorne between June and August carrying the ailing child with her.

Between the passing of the great and the wanderings of the poor and sick there were of course the ordinary travellers, who, stopping at the Crown Half Way House, or the Dover Castle, brought to the village news of the wider world so that it never suffered from the rural remoteness of so many villages in those centuries. What tales for instance did Hogarth and his companions tell on their visit to the Dover Castle (as recorded in his well known 'Peregrinations') when they drank three pots of beer. Later he was told that the place was 'an Evil House'.

Gads Hill at the eastern end of the Shorne portion of the Dover Road provided an element of lawlessness and danger for the traveller. It was during the seventeenth century that this 'high old robbing Place' gained its greatest notoriety. Shakespeare was not exaggerating when he placed his Falstaffian adventure on Gads Hill. It was from this spot that 'Swift Nick', the original of Dick Turpin, is said to have ridden to York in the time of Charles II. The crest of the hill was surrounded by the dense woodlands of Court Wood, Lambs Wood, Spaniard Wood and Pear Tree Wood, and was a place of violence, first reflected in local records by the entry in the parish registers which records the burial on the 4th November 1546 of 'Richard Stevens found slaine at Gaddes Hill Foote'.

Something of the scene is illustrated by a long report of Sir Roger Manwood (who with his interest in Shorne Manor at that time was able to speak from local knowledge) about incidents at Gads Hill in 1590.[1] In October he says there were robberies done on the hill by foot thieves, and upon the hue and cry being raised, one of the thieves named 'Zackfield' was found hiding in the bushes. In the months following he reports there were more robberies in the highways of Gads Hill and at Chatham Downs (east of Rochester), this time by horse thieves 'with such fat and lusty horses as were not like hackney horses or far journeying horses'. The gang committing these robberies was led by a man called 'Justice Graybeard' because he commonly wore a 'Vizard Graybeard'.

He goes on

'After the end of Michaelmas term three or four gentlemen from London riding home towards Canterbury at the west end of Gadshill were overtaken by five or six horsemen all in cloaks close up about their faces who . . . swiftly riding by them got to the east end of Gadshill and then turned about all their horses on the face of the true men, whereby they became in fear, but by chance one of the true men did know this Curtel . . . and after some speech between them of the manifold robberies there done . . . the five or six swift riders rode away to Rochester'.

Sir Roger ends his report with allegations about tippling houses where the robbers resorted. He does not name any of them, but the Dover Castle at the foot of Gads Hill, Hogarth's 'Evil House', was the nearest inn to the incidents he reports.

Sir Roger Manwood tells of what one might call the upper strata of highway robbery, but the Assize Records suggest that some of the villagers participated. Between 1568 and 1606 the Assizes dealt with five occasions when small groups of between two and five local men were charged with highway robbery on Gads Hill. They are usually described as labourers or husbandmen and one gets the impression that these were the ones that were caught, and that there was a substratum in the village which was quite ready to join in the activities on this 'robbing place'. Indeed the Assize rolls suggest that the bulk of the detected crime here was a purely local activity as few other cases of indictment for highway robbery at Gadshill are recorded.

The Dover Road is now widened and straightened so that it is hard to imagine its appearance in the seventeenth and eighteenth centuries, but, though now rebuilt, we have two memorials of those days in its wayside inns. First is The Crown Half Way House, now a garage, and the second is the Duke of York. This was formerly the Dover Castle, later the Angel, then the Anchor, and later still the Beef Steak House.

The Dover Castle may have been an 'Evil House' in Hogarth's time, but it was also part of the manor demesne and it was here that during the eighteenth century the manor court leet was held. The Crown Half Way House was apparently a coaching inn, and was frequently used by the overseers for their meetings. Unlike the Dover Castle, its name has remained unchanged from the seventeenth century. Many minor incidents of wayfarers falling sick or being in misfortune at the Crown appear in the two hundred years covered by our rate accounts, whilst on one occasion an overseer spent most of the day at the Crown waiting for the carrier and charged his 'expenses' on the rates.

These two inns were somewhat isolated, but the village was well served by other establishments. The See Ho on Shorne Ridgeway has a continuous history from the seventeenth century, when it was known as the 'So Ho', the earlier version of the hunting call from which it took its name. No doubt the name was associated with hunting in Cobham Park, half a mile to the south. From an old photograph of the place before it was burnt down in the 1890s (it was then re-

The 'Rose and Crown' public house, formerly 'The Crooked Billett', opened in 1734. This photograph was taken before recent brewer's 'restorations'.

built in Brewers' Victorian) it seems to have been a large building with an older building at the rear suggesting sixteenth century construction.

In the village, inns seem to have come and gone in steady profusion. All save one are now lost from living memory, and are but names to the local historian plodding through old records. For instance the manor rolls in 1684 mention 'The Hatchet' which seems later to have changed its name to 'The Wheatsheaf'. Today no one knows where the Wheatsheaf stood. In 1699 William Woodyear, the Lord of the manor, was rated for 'The King's Head'. It may have been the Dover Castle which changed its name frequently, but it seems unlikely. A similar uncertainty attached to a public house called the 'White Horse'. Throughout the seventeenth and eighteenth centuries this inn was most important. It is described in the manor rolls of 1684 as 'the messuage called The White Horse and the brewhouse stable and garden in Shorne Street, in the occupation of John Stone'. In 1781 the manor roll has a note that the place had been converted into three tenements whilst in a later roll some ten tenants are named, suggesting that the outbuildings had also been altered into tenements which was then a common use for all large properties. During its existence most of the parish vestries seem to have been held at this inn, yet today we have no certain information of where it stood. As a conjecture it may have been the present Post Office. Thong had an inn known as the 'Yorkshire Gray', which, when the White Horse in the Street ended its career, took the name of White Horse, and it is now White Horse Cottage.

The one inn in Shorne village which still remains, the Rose and Crown, has a fairly connected history. In 1736 Mr Taylor, the then Lord of the Manor, following the example set by his uncle William Woodyear, granted a long lease of a tenement in Pound Field, part of the manor demesne, and the lessee then rebuilt the tenement. There was at that time another inn in the village known as 'The Billett' whose whereabouts now are quite unknown. Mr French, who was then the licensee of The Billett, decided that the new house would make a better public house than the old Billett, so, without further ado, he removed his sign from the old Billett and hung it on the newly rebuilt house. In his hands the place seems to have settled down as the local village inn. However the rebuilding was rather shoddy — until recent brewers' improvements its east wall was supported by two enormous brick buttresses, and most of the inner filling of the exterior walls was block chalk. As can be seen today the brickwork on the front shifted, the courses being well out of alignment. Probably this is the reason why by the end of the eighteenth century it was known as 'The Crooked Billett'. In the early years of the nineteenth century its name was further changed to The Rose and Crown, and so it remains, the facade largely unaltered, but the interior now much changed and modernised into Brewers' Tudor.

During the recent alterations to this inn the stripping of the interior plaster revealed a small, much worn, child's shoe of eighteenth century date, carefully placed behind the plaster. The known date of the rebuilding agrees with the probable dating of the shoe.[2]

Another topographical feature of the village was its tanyards. The earliest tanyard of which we have any record is that at Little Moor on the Ridgeway, which was first noted in the hands of Jarvis Maplesden. Both the farmhouse Little Moors and the tanyards are now quite lost, but old maps show Little Moors as on the north side of the Ridgeway by a piece of waste which had a small pond known as Packs Pond. Recently when the field, the site of Little Moors, was ploughed, a complicated system of land drainage consisting of interlaced bullocks horns laid in long lines across the field was found, indicating a useful way of disposing of what must have been one of the tiresome by-products of tanning.

At the end of the seventeenth century the Little Moor tanyard passed into the hands of one George Startup, another tanner, who appears to have already had a tanyard also on the Ridgeway near Cooks Cross, or Chestnut corner as it is now called. This tanyard seems to have been approximately on the site of cottages now known as Park Cottages. It seems that George Startup, after acquiring Little Moors, allowed his old tanyard to fall into disuse, as a deed a hundred years later refers to the tanyard as long since demolished, and converted into two cottages. These two cottages stood behind the present Park Cottages and were recently demolished.

George Startup forms a link with another tanyard in the parish. In his will in 1720 he gave to his loving friend Thomas Tomlin, Tanner, a guinea in gold and a gold ring, and names him as overseer of his will.

The Tomlins were until almost living memory the tanners on the site of Tanyard House. The tanpits the family used still remain under the garden of the House, laid out as a sunken rose garden. It was formerly part of the Court Lodge grounds, and one would have thought that the occupiers of Court Lodge would have had enough of tanyards, which are not necessarily sweet neighbours, but strangely enough, there is some evidence to show that there was yet another tanyard even closer to the manor house. A lease of the Court Lodge estates by Mrs Gordon (the then lord of the manor) to Thomas Noakes in 1786 refers to a tanyard at the northernmost end of an oasthouse near Court Lodge. Probably this was in the somewhat swampy northern end of the Court Lodge gardens, and it seems likely that Thomas Noakes found it more pleasant to close the tanyard down, for it is not mentioned in sale particulars of the Court Lodge estate in 1815, though there was still a 'fellmongers yard' in the manor house yard.

All these tanyards no doubt owed their existence to the plentiful supply of soft water from the springs on the Ridgeway and nearby, with the oak bark freely available from the woods. As to the hides, the marshlands by the Thames provided almost endless grazing for the bullocks and sheep, whilst Cobham Park had its large herd of deer. When the foundations of an old barn were found in the field opposite the Little Moor tanyard site, an old villager recalled that his grandfather had told him that the barn was where they hung the deerskins from the park, awaiting tanning.

In the late seventeenth and early eighteenth century these deerskins formed the basis of another village industry which seems to have faded away during the eighteenth century. There were several glovers working in the village, and we may remember that deerskin gloves and gauntlets were the normal wear of the horseriding gentry and yeomanry.

1. Recorded by R.P. Cruden in his notes now at Gravesend Library.
2. Similar finds were made when plaster was removed from Mill Cottage on Shorne Hill, and from a house in the Street called Homemead Cottage. The Homewood Cottage shoe was about mid-nineteenth century. These are indications of an ancient long-continued custom recorded elsewhere in North Kent.

## Chapter 11
## THE LANDED GENTRY AND THEIR ESTATES

From the beginning of the seventeenth century interesting changes had been taking place in the ownership of the manors and the woods and fields of Shorne, and these form a background to the story, providing both family and topographical details of village affairs.

At the end of the sixteenth century the principal landowner in the village was William Brook, Lord Cobham, an important figure in Elizabethan England – Warden of the Cinque Ports, Lord Lieutenant of the County and much else. He was Lord of the manors of Shorne, Merston and Randall, and had the usual patriarchal interest of the great landowner in the communities under his sway, exemplified by his charitable foundation of Cobham College Almshouses and his annual gifts of 'Devocon money' to the parish.

On his death his estates passed to his son Henry Brook, Lord Cobham. On his being attainted for treason in the third year of the reign of James I the whole of his estates in Shorne and elsewhere escheated to the crown. King James soon distributed this windfall amongst his courtiers. Cobham Hall, Randall Manor and Merston Manor were granted to Ludovick Stuart, Duke of Lennox (later Duke of Richmond) whilst the manor of Shorne and its associated estate was granted to Robert Cecil, Earl of Salisbury, who sold the manor and lands to Sir John Leveson, whose brother later sold the whole to George Woodyear, an Alderman of Rochester, living at Satis House on Boley Hill at Rochester.

So begins a period of some two hundred years between the break-up of the wide possessions of the Lords of Cobham Hall in the parish, and the re-establishment of the Cobham Hall influence at the end of the eighteenth century and the beginning of the nineteenth century by the new Lords of Cobham Hall, the Earls of Darnley. During this period the manor and other estates in the village were owned and usually occupied by small local gentry and, for the first time that can be traced, the village had a resident Lord of the Manor.

Hitherto none of the manor lords had resided in the village and the manors and their estates seem normally to have been let. Of the tenants we have no record, except for Sir Roger Manwood the Elizabethan judge, who was the tenant of the manor at the end of the sixteenth century. Unlike most tenants he seems to have been responsible for various embellishments to the manor. If the stone bearing his name which was once incorporated in the walls is any guide, he was the builder of a complex of walls around the site of the old Shorne manor house in Shorne Street, and also the adjoining farm house known as Fullers. Even more important, he provided the village with its first public water supply. He built a small water tower on the hillside of what is now the land around Overblow House, which collected water from the several springs in the hillside, whence it was carried in a lead pipe to the manor house (now the site of three shops). Part of the supply was fed into a sunken cistern by the roadside nearby, with a pump for the villagers' use. The pump remained in use until the beginning of the twentieth century when modern piped water, company supplied, was put into the village, though the lead pipe still fed the water supply of a small nursery garden established within the walled area built by Sir Roger, until after the 1939/45 war.

From the churchwardens' accounts it seems that George Woodyear was living in the village during the 1630s at Court Lodge. This is the first reference to Court Lodge in any of the records which have survived, and it is probable that it was in fact originally a lodge attached to the manor for the use of the manor bailiff or steward. However from this time on, after some confusion during the next fifty years, it became the manor house. The older site in the Street became derelict, though sometimes used by the bailiff of the manor.

George Woodyear died in 1640 when his son and heir was a child. His widow Mary at once applied to the Court of Wards for the wardship of her son during his minority, not only in respect of the Manor of Shorne, but of lands in Cliffe and elsewhere in the county.

After he came of age, at some time in the 1660s, George Woodyear junior married Martha Haisden, daughter and heiress of George Haisden of Gravesend, who owned a considerable area of land in Shorne. According to the manor roll of 1684 the Haisden estates consisted of two houses: Shorne House and Brook Place (neither of which can be identified today), and 100 acres in Shorne and another 100 acres or so of land and two more houses on Shorne Ridgeway.

As a result of the marriage and the complicated laws of land ownership at the time this estate seems to have been treated as part of the estate of George Woodyear, for the manor rolls of both 1684 and 1702 each have a note against this entry 'In my Lord's hands', and this is supported by the terms of George Woodyear's will.

The marriage was a short one, but when George Woodyear died in 1671, his will gave his lands on Shorne Ridgeway to his daughter Mary, and Court Lodge, and 'the house I live in' and the lands belonging to Court Lodge to his son William. The will makes no reference to the manor with its commons, manorial rights, quit rents, demesne lands and woodlands, so we may assume that these were settled. Both William and Mary were minors, and their mother Martha took charge.

She seems to have been a strong-minded woman and does not seem to have been very pleased with the way in which her inheritance had been incorporated in the Woodyear estates. As soon as her daughter Mary married, and was thus able with her husband's cooperation to dispose of her inheritance under her father's will, she, with the consent of her husband (a Yorkshireman) sold back all her inheritance to her mother for the apparently small sum of £850, though the sale did not include the Shorne House and Brook Place parts of the Haisden estate.

From the time William Woodyear came of age we can trace the slow decline of the family fortunes. In 1691 he married an heiress in the person of Sarah, daughter of Sir Henry Greenhill of Plymouth. There were several children of this marriage, some of them baptised at Shorne Church, though 'Greenhill' Woodyear, the eldest son, seems to have been baptised elsewhere. Soon after his marriage William began to borrow money on the security of his inheritance, and Martha his mother began a series of piecemeal sales of the lands she had reacquired from her daughter. Beginning in 1697 a series of mortgages soon totalled over £2,000, so far as the documents survive, whilst Martha first sold the fields of Scammels, and the Downs at Shorne Ifield to Jarvis Maplesden, then some of the lands on the Ridgeway to the village publican John Stone (including the fields known since medieval times as 'Brighthaven' adjoining the See Ho), and then in 1699 she sold the remainder of her lands to Richard Buttenshaw.

When Greenhill Woodyear, the heir of the family, came of age, matters proved even more complicated. It appears that William Woodyear was the trustee of the estate of Sir Henry Greenhill, his father-in-law, and that young Greenhill Woodyear was the heir of his grandfather. On his coming of age later litigation reveals that the estate of Sir Henry Greenhill (totalling, according to the Court order, £13,911.2s.6¾d.), had in the hands of the trustees, been lost. To clear the indebtedness William Woodyear conveyed his mortgaged manorial estates at Shorne to his son at the price of the court's estimate of the value of the estate of Sir Henry Greenhill's estate. The transaction was completed in 1711, but during the following years Greenhill Woodyear followed his father's example by further mortgages of the estate and on his death in 1722 without an heir the whole heavily encumbered estate reverted to his father.

Martha Woodyear died in 1720 and left to himself William Woodyear continued to nibble away at his estates. He began a policy of granting long leases of small portions to builders, though because of the uncertainty of description it is not possible to conjecture where the buildings were. One example however is clear. In 1731 he granted land, part of Court Lodge Farm, an orchard and Fen field to Thomas Tomlin a tanner. This land surrounded the present Tanyard House, and because of the slackness of the later owners of the manor finally became freehold in the Tomlin family, and no part of the old manorial holdings.

On the death of William Woodyear, the whole of his estates passed to his niece Catherine Page and then to his nephew John Taylor. Something of the confusion of William Woodyear's affairs is reflected in a Deed of Arrangement between Catherine Page and John Taylor in 1733, the year after William Woodyear's death. Lengthy recitals record that after paying the interest on the loans and other charges on the estate the net income available was only £174 a year, and that William Woodyear's unsecured debts exceeded his personal estate by the sum of £855.11.4½d.

After Catherine Page's death in 1736 John Taylor lived in Shorne for a few years, but finally in 1747 the manor and the whole of the surviving estate was put on the market, though it was not until 1753 that it was sold to Mr Thomas

Gordon, a merchant of London, for £9,000. Thus the Woodyear connection with the village ended.

Whilst the Woodyear's fortunes were declining, other families in the village were expanding their influence and acres. By far the most important and influential family in the village was that of the Maplesdens. The family was an old Kentish one with branches in Rochester and Maidstone, but the first of whom we have record as living in the parish was Jarvis Maplesden who in about 1620 came to Little Moor on Shorne Ridgeway, where he either took over an existing tannery, or established a new one.

In 1622 he married Margaret Edmets. They had eight children of whom some daughters and two sons Jarvis and George survived. The original Jarvis early began to partake regularly in parish affairs, serving from time to time in all the parish offices, and generation after generation his descendants followed his example. When he died in 1645 he seems to have been the owner of about thirty acres of land around Little Moor and whatever the family pretensions to gentility, he would by the standards of the times be still only in the yeoman class.

On their father's death the two brothers continued his tannery, no doubt very profitably at the time of the New Model Army and the powerful Cromwellian Navy, both of which required large quantities of leather.

Jarvis II, as already mentioned in Chapter 8, was an active vestry man during the later years of the Interregnum, and held a Captain's commission in the militia. After the Restoration he began to expand his activities beyond the tannery, which seems to have been left in the hands of his brother. He purchased a small estate in Shorne Ifield described in the manor rolls of 1684 as 'A messuage called Ifield Place and several pieces of land containing about 45 acres' with other adjoining fields called Ashenden and West Lambers. He also became steward of the Duke of Richmond of Cobham Hall. A number of his letters to the Duke survive in the archives of the British Museum among the Richmond Papers. These letters reveal that much of the management of the Cobham estate and the alterations to Cobham Hall were in Jarvis Maplesden's capable hands. They contain references to deer poaching in Cobham Park, and additions being made to Cobham Hall, which seems at that time to have been a half-empty shell of a building in which lurking wayfarers could be found. Even more unusual are the references to the Duke's privateer which Jarvis Maplesden seems to have managed when in port. Jarvis II also has the distinction of a passing mention in Pepys' Diary when the diarist mentions the acquisition of timber for the navy through Jarvis Maplesden. Probably this was timber from the Duke's park and it marks the dockyard and naval connections which Jarvis had developed.

They were a prolific family. Jarvis II married twice and Jarvis III was born in 1657 followed by nine brothers and sisters, many of whom did not survive childhood. Making confusion for the genealogist, George, Jarvis II's brother, married in 1660 and in that year Jarvis II christened his second son George, whilst George Maplesden senior in 1662 had a son whom he also christened George. To add to these genealogical difficulties there appears to have been a 'cousinage' of branches of the family which, though not living in the village, kept close touch with the Shorne connection.

One of the 'cousinage', Margaret Maplesden, married John Baynard of Shorne Ifield. The Baynard family and fortunes thread their way through this history. We have already met an earlier John Baynard who was appointed a 'collector for the poor' in 1598. At that time he was the farmer of some forty acres of land in the Shorne Ifield area, and we may safely assume he lived at the cottage at Shorne Ifield still called 'Baynards'. He also owned land at Bickley and marshland called Rosehope and Colchester Hope on the Shorne/Higham boundary. In 1614 he purchased from one Richard Walton of Leysdown a house, barns and buildings, garden, orchard, woodland and arable land in Shorne, in all some hundred acres. The deeds which have survived give long lists of field names now long lost – Boydendean, Brookfield, Wevills, Huttocks Corner, Agnes Agate, and so on, all fragments of another age with their centre around Thong Lane. An interesting point about this purchase is that it does not seem to have comprised land in any way part of the manor of Shorne. Quit rent is paid to the manor for the original holding, but not the purchased land, which may well have been part of the lands of the original Randall manor.

In his title deeds and on his tombstone in Shorne churchyard (the earliest identifiable grave outside the church) old John Baynard proudly describes himself as 'Yeoman', but as the generations pass with expanding acres the attributes of gentility attached to the family. Two fine eighteenth century black memorial slabs in Shorne church chancel not only mark the last resting place of a later John Baynard, but also the rise in status, the later John Baynard being described as 'Gentleman of Rochester'.

By the time of his death Jarvis II had undoubtedly established the fortunes of the family on a secure basis, both by his business ability, and the family connections, with the Baynard estate adjoining his own in Shorne Ifield. On his death in 1681 he was accorded the accolade of 'Gent' in the registers, and was buried in the north chancel of the church where his black slate memorial slab records his last resting place and proudly displays his arms 'Sable, a cross fermee, fitches' (according to Hasted).

He was succeeded by his son Jarvis III who was 24 years of age when his father died, and who in 1684 married Jane Paine of Northfleet. His first son Jarvis IV was born in 1685. We have already met Jarvis III as one of the trustees appointed to hold the parish field when it was finally bought with the Page legacy, and he was to be a regular attendant at the vestries, though he does not appear to have taken office of any description. He continued the family policy of extending the lands of the family, acquiring, as we have already noted, Scammels and Upper and Lower Downs from Martha Woodyear, all adjoining the Ifield Place lands. Early in the eighteenth century he also acquired from the Parker family the old house of Pipes Place, with some twenty acres of land including the old chapel of St Katherines and Burrow or Barrow Hill.

Pipes Place, the former home of the Maplesden family.

Shortly after his acquisition of Pipes Place Jarvis III died, to be succeeded by his son Jarvis IV who had married one Jane before his father's death and was able to tell his father before he died that the line would continue with the birth of the fifth Jarvis in 1706, when to make the matter quite clear the registers record the baptism of 'The son of Gervayse Maplesden Jn Gent'. Jarvis IV however only survived his father by some ten years, dying in 1716 at the early age of 34 leaving his widow Jane to bring up four children, with another born after his death.

At this point another Shorne family comes into the Maplesden connection. In a previous chapter we have mentioned Thomas Ayerst, the vicar from 1670 to 1688, who soon after coming to the parish had married one of the Maplesden 'cousinage'. They had several children, the most important of whom from the point of view of this history was William Ayerst, born in 1685. William followed his father's profession, being ordained into the ministry and becoming a Doctor of Divinity. He was, however, no ordinary parish clergyman, but was attached as chaplain and secretary to various embassies in the reigns of Queen Anne and George I. His memorial in Canterbury Cathedral with the usual verbosity of a funeral memorial says he was 'of distinguished ability and merit both as a divine and master of business' and he was rewarded for his services with a prebend at Canterbury which he held until his death.

In spite of his services abroad the Rev. Dr Ayerst retained his association with the village in which he had been born and with his Maplesden cousins. So, shortly after the death of Jarvis IV, the Rev. William Ayerst married Jarvis's widow Jane, and during the next few years four children of the marriage were born, one of whom, Robert Gunsley Ayerst, not only followed his father as a Doctor of Divinity, but, as we shall see later, maintained the family connection with Shorne.

In 1735 the Rev. Dr William Ayerst acquired from the trustees of William Downs of Chatham the substantial farm in the centre of Shorne known as Fullers. It consisted of the broad fields by Swillers Lane and beyond bounding the Pipes Place estate on two sides. It included two woods which can still be identified, Star Wood and Cole Wood on the Ridgeway, and

> 'Also a little piece of meadow through which passeth a stream of water called the Bottom being the lower side of Fullers or Greenfield 1½ acres on which piece of meadow formerly stood a water mill'.

The farmhouse itself was on the side of Shorne Hill opposite the churchyard entrance, and had formerly been the home of the Page family. By the time the Rev. Ayerst purchased it the old house was dilapidated, having for a time at the end of the seventeenth century been used as a victualling house known as The Swan. The Rev. Ayerst (Hasted says Mrs Ayerst) rebuilt or largely restored this old house. Only the substantial cellars now remain, buried beneath garden ground.

Thus the Maplesden-Ayerst connection in the village formed a large block of land in the parish. The only divergence from the Maplesden policy of increasing acreage was when George Maplesden, who had taken over the Little Moor Farm and tannery on Shorne Ridgeway, left that property to his sons Thomas and John who sold it to George Startup, another 'tanner'.

Jane Ayerst and her second husband were trustees of the estate of Jarvis IV on behalf of the heir Jarvis V who took possession of his estate on attaining his majority in 1727. He left the local historian an unexpected bonus. On his coming of age he compiled a vellum notebook carefully recording the money and real estate which he inherited, with details of his marriages, the dowries he received with each wife, and a list of his children.

Before he came of age Jarvis V had (in 1725) married Elizabeth the daughter of Richard Watts of Rochester, and her dowry is noted as £100. The wedding was in September and in June the following year the expected heir Jarvis VI was born. Elizabeth died in 1728, and a year later the young widower married Diana, daughter of Benjamin Crayker of Farningham. She died at the birth of their only child Benjamin in 1731, and the following year Jarvis married for the third time, this time Rachel, daughter of Lewis Lett of Gravesend. Her dowry is recorded as £350 and on the death of Lewis Lett she was apparently his heir and Jarvis Maplesden records that he received, by right of his wife, three assorted mortgages. One for £1,000 was charged on the estates of George Gordon of Rochester, the second was for £250 owing by one William Halfinder of Gravesend, and the third was for £50 due from one John Turner of Gravesend described as a tilt boat master.

Jarvis also acquired from his father-in-law's estate a fascinating collection of clothes and personal equipment which he carefully recorded in the note book. We shall meet him on many occasions in later chapters, and he will perhaps become a little more real if we allow ourselves to wonder if on any of those occasions he was wearing one of the three wigs, one of the six silk shirts, the double breasted great coat or the close bodied coat with black buttons. Did he prefer the black tabby waistcoat, or the light coloured cloth coat lined with blue silk, and which pair of breeches — the black or the drab? Did he use the silver watch, three rings, silver shoe buckles, the saddle, bridle and whip, which are all so carefully listed in the note book?

All this affluence — and the large family which grew up around him and his third wife — was probably the reason for his rebuilding Pipes Place, which assumed its present Georgian form during Jarvis V's lifetime, though somewhat surprisingly he makes no mention of it in his notebook.

Yet by the time of his death in 1769 Jarvis V must have realised that the continuity of the line was likely to be broken. Jarvis VI married one Anne of whom we know nothing, but had no children. It is said he was in the Royal Navy and became governor of Greenwich Hospital, but the old family confusion returns at this point with collaterals at West Malling, one of whom was called Captain Jarvis Maplesden in the will of Jarvis V.

From this point the story of the Maplesdens recedes from the foreground of village history, but after the burial of Jarvis II in the north chancel of the church the family continued to bury its dead there generation after generation, and though most of the worn slabs are covered by the organ we may recall that in 1812, long after the last Jarvis had gone from the scene, the vicar made a note in the registers that John Venner the parish clerk had affirmed 'that the part of the chancel out of the vestry had always been repaired by the Maplesden family'. Otherwise the only part of the church to be particularly associated with a family is the Randall Chapel, erected by the proud medieval lord centuries before.

## Chapter 12
## THE POOR AND THE OVERSEERS

After the beginning of the poor law in the village, described in Chapter 7, for the next century and a half the story continued with only minor variations, but the village records are so full of detail during that period that a further study of life in the lower strata of village affairs seems a proper continuation after the story of the landed gentry told in the last chapter. Here poor children are fostered and apprenticed, the sick are nursed, treated and relieved, the widows and aged and 'impotent' folk are paid weekly sums, housed and buried at the end of their days, and the story introduces not only the poor but the officers of the parish who administered the whole business, without pay, and often it would seem without any previous training.

One part of the relief of the poor which is rather separate from the main background is the apprenticeship of children, and has its own story. Some ninety-six indentures of apprenticeship survive among the parish archives. Of these, forty-seven belong to the seventeenth century and the parish accounts suggest there may have been more which are now lost. Examination of the indentures discloses the general idea behind the system. Among the forty-seven deeds, there are only eleven which provide for the apprentice to be taught a 'trade' such as bricklayer, carpenter, glover, or the like. One is of particular interest in a history of the village. In 1654 Thomas Essex was apprenticed to Thomas Williams of Shorne (he was the local blacksmith) who is described in the Indenture as 'Gunsmith', to learn the 'art trade mystery or occupation of a gunsmith'. This is an unexpected trade in a rural community where the only other industry besides agriculture was tanning, and reminds us of the possibility of other activities in the parish of which no records have survived.

Of the remaining thirty-six indentures, there are six for 'lawful labour and employment', seven for 'husbandry', two for 'honest labour and husbandry' and three for 'housewifery'. The remainder give vague variations of these 'trades' or mention no specific employment at all. Two of the girls' indentures are of interest in that they specify a little more fully what was considered to be 'housewifery'. In one the apprentice was to be taught to 'knit spin and all other housewifely duties fit for such an apprentice' and the other is to be taught 'all manner of household and country business' by the man of the house and 'knitting spinning etc' by his wife.

The deeds contain the quaint provisions and phraseology which have persisted in some formal trade apprenticeship deeds almost into living memory. The boy was bound by formal covenants to serve and the master to teach: the apprentice, if a boy, covenants to behave himself, but if a girl this covenant is omitted and the master simply covenants that she 'should not through idleness fall into ill courses'. Presumably the covenant of a female not to misbehave was not worth the parchment it was written on. Finally the master covenanted to fit the apprentice out at the end of the term with two suits of clothes, one for work and the other suitable for holidays or (as some deeds have it) 'Fit for Lord's day'.

At the beginning of the term it was normal for the parish to supply the apprentice with suitable clothing, and the accounts contain many examples of the general outfit which a child received at this, the beginning of his career. For example Thomas Goodwin was bound to William Cooke, a Glover of Dartford in 1675 at a premium of £6,

| | |
|---|---|
| 'Paid for the cure of Tho. Goodwyns head | £2. 10. 0. |
| (This seems to have been a common preliminary to apprenticeship, and suggests dirty and infested conditions.) | |
| 'Paid Will. Cotman for 2 suits and 2 waistcoats for Goodwyn | £1. 13. 0. |
| 'Paid for a hatt and stockings and shoes and bands for Goodwyn | 10. 0. |
| 'Paid to John Stone for carrying of Goodwyn to Dartford | 2. 0.' |

John Stone (a victualler) seems to have fostered the lad for a time, and it is a pity, after marking the boy riding away with John Stone in his new finery, to find an entry in 1678 'Paid for a warrant to remove Thos Goodwyn. 1.0d'. Evidently the child (he was only about nine years old) had run away from his master at Dartford and returned to the village in which he had been born, only to be sternly ejected by the overseers, because not only did his apprenticeship bind him to serve until he was twenty-four years of age, but it settled him in Dartford — a most important consideration to the overseers of Shorne. It does suggest however that the lad had been happy, if dirty, in the foster-parentage of John Stone before he was apprenticed.

Not all apprentices went out of the village. During the seventeenth century a sort of roundsman's system called the 'custom of Shorne' grew up. Villagers were apparently required to take children by some unexplained system of rotation. Probably it was a way of getting some small payment for apprenticeship out of the rates, and getting cheap servants. For instance Rejoice Head, an overseer, took his own niece as an apprentice with a premium of £3.

Occasionally the overseers took steps to get a boy off to sea. Entries like

| | |
|---|---|
| 'Paid George Howard's wife to carry her two boys on board a ship to try and get them masters | 6d.' (1700) |
| or | |
| 'Paid for fitting of Conyers boy for two gow to see | 15. 0.' (1709) |

suggest that the grey river and the brave sails on it drew the adventurous country lad.

The care of the sick was an important (and expensive) part of the poor law administration. Nursing and treatment not only of the sick villager, but the sick wayfarer was a steady and often quite expensive charge on the rates. A doctor's fees were generally between two and three pounds, whilst the services of a village woman to nurse the invalid generally came to several shillings a week. Apart from weekly payments for nursing, there were the 'salves' and 'cures' which generally cost five or six shillings each, and the patient often had further comforts in the shape of special foods and drink. Brandy and wine occasionally appear as medicine.

The most common illness mentioned is smallpox. Every year there are references to this sickness. Strangers brought it to the village and were housed in the public houses or the barns in and around the village. The accounts form a roll call of the barns and farms in the parish. 'Mr Richmonds barn', 'Mr Reeds barn', 'my stables', 'Mr Maplesden's barn', 'Mrs Terrys', 'Mr Gordons house', 'Kings Farm', 'Mr Cadwells barn', 'Birds', 'Mr Days house', 'Mr Jones barn', 'Mr G. Maplesdens barn'; all are mentioned, some of them more than once.

There was little distinction between the treatment of a villager and a stranger in misfortune, except that the stranger was got out of the parish as quickly as possible. For instance in 1708 'a stranger' broke his leg at the Half Way House. The overseer sent off a man on horseback to Strood for a surgeon, paying the surgeon £3 for setting the man's leg, and then providing 'stilts for carrying him to Gravesend with money victuals and drink to send him to London', no doubt on the Tilt boats of the Long Ferry.

This compares with the story of William Wellard, a villager. He was one of three brothers, Thomas, William and Valentine, of whom we have already met Thomas doing repairs to the church. William Wellard married one Sarah Reeve and lived as the tenant of a small holding at Thong owned by John Baynard, described in the manor roll as 'a messuage yard and five dayworks of land at Thong'. His marriage was a fruitful one with some six children of whom the first was born five months after his marriage. Whilst his family was growing William and his wife seem to have been among the villagers who were regularly employed to foster orphan children of the parish. In 1680 he kept 'John Payses child' for eight weeks at half a crown a week, and a girl of 'Goodwife Hotte' at a similar rate. The next year he was employed by the parish for an unpleasant-sounding job.

'Paid to William Wellard for taking a stranger up after he was
burried and a blankett to wrap him in                                    2. 0.'

Apart from these odd employments he was never relieved by the rates, and indeed in 1694 he is noted as being rated for 'The Hauth' which it seems was a field of some 10 acres fronting on the old Roman road near Clay Lane Woods.

In 1699 however, disaster overtook him, best described in the entries in the rate accounts:

'Paid Embersons wife for being at and helping Wellard in his
lameness                                                                 2. 0.
'Gave Widd. Wellard when her husbands legg was cut off she
being in distress                                                        5. 0.
'Pd Mr Hogg and Mr Withers for cutting off Wm Wellards legg
and expenses for Mr Maplesden and myself when we treated
with them for doing the same                                             5.14. 0.

'Paid John Terry for a coffin for William Wellard being very large 9. 0.
'Paid Holding for helping Terry carry the coffin to Thong 6. 0.
'Paid the clerks fee for burying Wellard 4. 0.'

William Wellard was in his fifties when he died, and one wonders at the description 'being very large'. Was he a giant, or only vastly obese?

William Wellard was perhaps a special case, but the village records sometimes enable us to trace a long period of a villager's life, reflecting the life and ideas of the times. For instance the activities, in sickness and in health, of Goode Davis can be traced over a period of nearly thirty years, and are worth recording for the light they throw on the activities of the poor law overseers of the time.

The Davis family was an old village family, but because of the gaps in the registers during the Civil War we have no record of the marriage of Thomas Davis, nor the date of his death. There are two entries of baptism, of Margaret Davis in 1643 and Alice Davis in 1651, as daughters of Thomas Davis, both in the old register which we assume was retained by the Revd Balam during the Civil War, but the first clear information we have about the Widow Davis is in the poor law accounts of 1657 when she occupied one of the parish cottages, built on Shorne Common some fifty years before. In 1654 and 1655 two daughters of Widow Davis were 'put out' as apprentices by the parish, but the youngest daughter Alice still lived with her in the cottage.

From these small events it appears that Thomas Davis had died between the birth of his youngest daughter in 1651 and the apprenticing of his eldest daughter in 1654, and that in 1657 Goode Davis was a widow of middle age, with only the parish and her own activities to support her. During the years which followed she appears as a pauper, village nurse, and one might almost surmise the village white witch.

In 1657 and the following years she seems to have suffered some undefined illness and had trouble with her leg, as each year she was treated by Mr Ceaser, the surgeon from Rochester, at the cost to the parish of two bills of 18s.6d. and 17s.6d. During this period she received a weekly payment of one shilling and sixpence, a payment which went on for three to four years. In 1662 however the weekly payments cease, apparently because she was then earning a living as a nurse, often employed by the overseers. In 1665 they paid her twelve shillings for 'looking to old Goodwyn' for two weeks, and later another six shillings for nursing him yet again. The next year she was 'looking to' one Black John for eight weeks at three shillings a week, receiving another one shilling and sixpence for 'laying him forth' on his death. In 1668 she nursed Old Goodwyn for the last time and 'laid him forth'.

The next year she is concerned with one Mary Jennings, who had trouble with her leg, when she was coupled with a doctor from Rochester both 'looking to Mary Jennings legg'. Unfortunately neither did Mary Jennings much good, for we find her later called the 'lame maid' or 'Lame Mary' in the accounts as she limped her way through the next few years with the frequent help of Widow Davis and the parish, evidenced by such entries as:

'Paid more to Mary Jennings when she was sick and to Goodwife
   Davis for salves for her and for looking to her              £1. 5. 0.'

until in 1675 there are the usual entries recording the death and burial of Mary Jennings.

During these years Widow Davis is quite highly paid for her nursing, salves, and 'cures'. Such items as a payment of three pounds 'concerning Mary Jennings head' or another ten shillings 'towards the cure of John Axells tooe' (though this seems to have done him little good as a little later in the same account she was paid the usual one shilling and six pence for 'laying him forth') show that she was in regular demand by the parish officers, and no doubt had a private practice as well among the more well-to-do villagers. She seems to have continued to occupy the parish cottage all this time.

In 1677 she fell sick, the overseers paying her two shillings and six pence 'when she was sick', and she was paid the whole of a fine of five shillings which the overseers had received that year from 'the miller for not coming to church'. Next year she had an accident and for a year or so she received odd amounts of weekly relief, until finally in 1680 we take leave of the old lady in the entries.

'Paid for carring Wid. Davis goods to Cobham                   3. 0.
'Paid Tho. Wellard for wood for Wid. Davis and mending
   her bedsteadall when she went to Cobham                    5. 4.'

With her move to Cobham Almshouses we lose trace of this active old lady but we may well imagine her doctoring or nursing, so far as she was able, the other inmates of the college.

The overseers occasionally raised funds by the sale of a pauper's goods, which give us an insight into the furnishings of the poor villager when the receipts are sometimes listed in full. The sales seem to have been by auction after they had been 'Cried' around the village by the parish clerk. When Widow Harpe's goods were sold, the overseers listed what was sold, the price, and interestingly, who bought them.

'Received of Mrs Ayerst for one little feather bedd and pillows
   and 3 old blanketts and 2 old coverlidds and some odd things    £2. 8. 0.
'Recd for 2 old sacks and one old bit halter and an old
   lanthorne                                                                2. 2.
'Recd of Mr Swindon for one old flock bed and 2 bolsters and
   bedstead                                                            12. 0.
'Recd for some trenchers and an old scummer and a seive and
   odd things                                                        3. 6.
'Recd of Goodwife Hunt and Goodwife Hubbards and
   Goodwife Paine for things                                 £1. 2. 0.'

Thus are recorded the humble belongings of Widow Harpe and the curious fact that a large part was bought by Mrs Ayerst the widow of the former vicar, and the Revd Swindon, the vicar at that time.

On a later occasion one Dame Judd came on the rates and her furniture was sold, but this time before selling it the overseers got Mr Reed to 'Prize' the goods and paid someone for cleaning and mending her clock and clock case. At the sale the clock fetched £2.15s.0d., and 'Dame Jud's Puter' thirteen shillings. This suggests the lady had a somewhat better home than the usual pauper. A little later Dame Judd came into the accounts again in another aspect of parish relief which occasionally occurs in the accounts. Just after Christmas the overseers paid £1.5s.0d. for a license, and seven shillings and sixpence for marrying her, giving her a guinea as a wedding present, and garnishing the wedding celebrations with a leg of mutton costing two shillings and sixpence.

A way of keeping down expenses was the withdrawal of payments from most of those receiving weekly benefits during the season of harvest, and in Shorne there were, in those days, two harvests, cherrytime and the normal corn harvest. In the parish there were as far as we can now trace some one hundred and thirty acres of cherry trees.[1] The picking of this large acreage seems to have been as much of a communal activity as the ordinary harvest, all able-bodied villagers and some not so able-bodied being drawn into the two or three weeks of cherry picking.

This special village activity is mentioned in the trouble which seems to have arisen with one of the overseers. In 1684 we find the accounts of John Stone the overseer corrected by the striking out of one item of 'charges of carring the Howes to Maidstone £1' and a note at the end of the accounts by the magistrates:

> 'Memorandum Yt Henry Mills says yt he hath two shillings a week but for 8 weeks and for the rest of the year but one shilling per week (excepting cherry time and harvest when he had nothing) and Richard Holder affirming yt he had nothing from cherry time till Michaelmas of wch John Stone is to give an account.'

The magistrate's memorandum is struck out in the book and the name John Stone is heavily (but unsuccessfully) erased, suggesting that the overseer had got his hands on the account book again and in a temper struck out the memorandum.

The accounts in fact show that John Stone had credited himself with the payment to Henry Mills of two shillings a week for the whole year and in the same way credited a whole year at a shilling a week as paid to Richard Holden, and the episode illustrates the care with which the accounts were checked by the magistrates. John Stone was the maltster and the son of John Stone the innkeeper at the White Horse, who had taken Thomas Goodwyn the apprentice to Dartford only a few years before. The family was among the more wealthy in the village, so this minor 'fiddling' seems hard to believe. John Stone wrote his own accounts and his phonetic spelling enables us faintly to catch the accents of villagers in that age. He pays Widow Warren to 'nus' several people. 'Ar pons' are purchased for several 'garls' in the village, and he makes his 'Arthur David' before the magistrates.

1. One imagines that the cries of 'cherry ripe' in the London streets often referred to Shorne cherries.

## Chapter 13
## AN EIGHTEENTH CENTURY VICAR

After the death of the Revd Thomas Ayerst in 1688 the Revd Tobias Swindon became vicar, and he was followed by his son, the Revd Tobias Clifton Swindon in 1719. Neither vicar made much mark in parish affairs; they both used the then fashionable Dog Latin in the registers, and the second Tobias lived in the vicarage or Cross House.

The first Tobias Swindon was a pluralist holding the Rectory of Cuxton jointly with his living at Shorne, and when he died the Revd Caleb Parfect became Rector of Cuxton, and on the vacancy in the Shorne living, caused by the death or transfer of the second Tobias Clifton Swindon, the Revd Caleb Parfect was inducted into the living of Shorne also, and held both livings until his death in 1770.

Mr Parfect was ordained in 1715 by the Bishop of Gloucester but seems to have had some influence in the appointments of Rochester Diocese, since the living at Cuxton was in the gift of the Bishop of Rochester. At the same time he became a minor canon at Rochester and was inducted into the vicarage of Strood which was in the gift of the Dean and Chapter of Rochester. Two livings in one year from two different patrons from the same diocese implies some strong influence working on his behalf.

Influence or not, it is clear he had no intention of living the life of an absentee pluralist. He developed a habit of leaving notes and copies of letters on all sorts of subjects scattered over the registers of the parishes of which he was incumbent as well as keeping tithe books copiously annotated with comments about the parishioners and their doings, all of which make him the local historian's great friend. His activities at Strood are well recorded in 'Smetham's History of Strood', and it may well be assumed that by the time he was inducted at Shorne some of his ideas about payment of tithes, parish morality and the care of the poor had spread to the village.

From his notes we know something of what he thought of the village he came to in 1733. His first impression of the vicarage is recorded in a letter he wrote many years later:

> 'Mr Parfect after he had been vicar a year or two of this parish had a great desire to reside at it the summer half of the year tho' it had no good reputation for its healthiness. He was therefore obliged to be at a large expense to make the vicarage house (one of the meanest and most minor cottages in the place and never inhabited by the vicar except a very few years by the last) a tolerable dwelling for himself and family.'

In spite of his doubts about its healthiness Mr Parfect and his family resided at the old vicarage every summer for the rest of his life, noting in his tithe book year by year the exact dates of his arrival and departure each year, and though he spent the winter months at Rochester he kept a lively and sardonic eye on the village and its affairs, making copious notes in his tithe book, the parish registers and other parish books which bring the village and its people vividly before us.

From the moment of his coming into the living Mr Parfect was concerned to see that he was getting the full value to which he was entitled. One matter which early concerned him was the glebe lands belonging to the living, and from his recorded actions in this connection we have a lot of incidental information about now lost features, and the activities of some of its inhabitants.

There were then three pieces of glebe in the parish. One was 'near Martyns', which was on the parish boundary between Park Pale and the Ridgeway road where it joined the old Roman road, the second piece was in Crown Lane apparently divided by the tithe barn belonging to the rectorial tithes, and the third was a narrow strip near Swillers Lane, still identifiable to the east of Warren View. Mr Parfect also looked upon the churchyard as being his freehold to produce what it might by way of pasturage.

His first concern was the Swillers plot. It had a considerable disability in that there was no clear means of access to it. It was surrounded on all sides by the fields of Fullers Farm belonging to the Revd Dr William Ayerst, Mr Maplesden's stepfather. Part of this farm on the north side of the glebe was the disused watermill, with its millpond and mill dam, all roughly on the site of the present Swillers Farm buildings. All the time the vicar let the glebe to the tenant of Fullers Farm the question of access did not arise, but with a characteristic cantankerousness, Mr Parfect turned the old tenant out of the glebe land soon after he took over the living, and the access, across the Fullers barn yard (which was at the junction of Swillers Lane with Shorne Street), and thence through Greenfield (where Warren View now stands), was challenged. A lengthy, and sometimes acrimonious, correspondence followed between the two clerics, which Mr Parfect preserved, and it supplies unexpected sidelights on village life and topography.

The mill pond was, it seems, partially dried out and was known as 'Springs', 'Ox's Field' (Ox was a village shop keeper) or 'Spots'. Swillers Lane was a well established highway, and the old mill dam crossed the shallow valley from Swillers Lane to the eastern corner of the glebe. Mr Parfect's new tenant not only kept a cow and a horse on the glebe, but as Mr Parfect says 'keeping a public house and being a cricketer he now and then carries young men thither to play at that game'. To get there they apparently crossed Greenfield and Mr Warren, the farmer tenant of the Revd Ayerst, objected, though as Mr Parfect observes, he often permitted cricket to be played on his fields.

Mr Parfect found a village ancient, one John Nichols, who having made a lengthy declaration that the glebe had always been reached by passing through Fullers barnyard, then died. In return the vicar noted 'I gave him a funeral sermon', an easy posthumous reward. Ultimately an agreement was reached that

Mr Ayerst should grant Mr Parfect and his tenant a right of way over the old mill dam, Mr Parfect to put in a proper culvert.

Whilst this dispute was going on, Mr Parfect reorganised his tithes. It must be remembered that in those days the incumbent's income was literally one tenth of the crops and products of the parish fields, and because this was incredibly difficult to collect in specie it was normal for the incumbent to agree a payment in cash called a 'modus' or 'composition' instead of the tenth turnip, gallon of milk, or egg. So when a new parson came to a parish he found himself faced with a series of 'moduses' agreed by his predecessor, which because of improved production or higher prices represented nothing like a tenth of the value of the product of the field, but which was always urged by the tithepayer as 'customary' and therefore unchangeable.

Mr Parfect never liked the system, and indeed at Strood had taken a tenth of the milk of one of his tithepayers, and a tenth bushel of the hops of another to prove his point. In a letter to Mr Gordon, the then Lord of the Manor, some years later he observes:

'You will see . . . how much we are obligated to look out for and pick up every little affair − and it is a disgrace to ye nation yt every clergyman's provision for himself and family should arise so great a part of it in so mean and unbecoming a manner.'

Nevertheless he was quite willing to 'pick up every little affair' and as a result we have a wide picture of the village farming and minor products, derived from his constant reconnoitring of the parish and its fields. Fruit, cherries, pears and apples figure frequently, the crops varying from year to year. In 1754 he notes 'a great deal of fruit and he (Thomas Tomlin) promises to send me some − did so'. Hops were another crop which he watched with a strict eye, arguing with the grower about the acreage. Turnips were a crop mentioned frequently, whose tithe Mr Parfect pursued diligently. For instance one year he notes:

'Mr Bilboe (the miller at the time) has a great crop of turnip seed to account for, it is said to amount to 10 quarters and a bushel ? how much sold for p. bushel − hardly under half a guinea − the tenth part of the money is due abating for threshing marketing etc.'

These complicated considerations give some idea of the problem and Mr Parfect finally settled for £3.5s.0d. composition with Mr Bilboe.

Forage crops of Sainfoin, Clover, Ryegrass, and Lucerne were common and peas appear to have been grown as a field crop, though potatoes were only grown as a garden crop and so not titheable. From the tithe book we learn that there was a willow plat growing in the marshy ground by Swillers, and Mr Parfect collected a tithe of the withies. Animals were titheable; a cow and calf at 2s.0d. and two calves at 2s.0d.

The mixed nature of a villager's occupation is well enough illustrated by Mr Parfect's notes. For instance Mr Lawrence kept the Beef Steak House (it is worth noting that the older name of the Dover Castle had changed by 1763), but he also kept two cows and a horse, and grew three yards of hops. Mr Lampard, a small farmer called by Mr Parfect in one of his notes 'wrongheaded Lampard', not only kept pigs – and gave Mr Parfect one of the piglets – but also carried two loads of hay to Rochester and acted as a carrier to Mr Parfect on one or two of his peregrinations between Shorne and Rochester in the spring and autumn. Later the tithe book notes that he was 'broke and fled'.

Misfortune of one sort or another has always gone on behind the curtain of formal history, but it is interesting when, for a moment, Mr Parfect lifts the curtain for insignificant people of whom we have no other record, noting in his tithe book in 1757 that William Sandrock had had a bad year. He farmed a field of clover of which he only harvested two and a half acres; he had a farrow of pigs 'but ye sow died'; three cows and two calves 'but one of the cows died'. 'Under these misfortunes took 9s. for the whole' Mr Parfect notes.

Mr Parfect did not confine his arguments over tithes to the poorer members of the parish. At Cuxton he had a famous quarrel with Lord Darnley about tithes in that parish which reached the law courts, and in which he was successful. In Shorne he wrote long and quite exasperated letters to Mr Day, the farmer of Kings Farm in Lower Shorne, because he sold his crops before Mr Parfect could inspect them. 'You have sold my tithe' he exclaims in one letter.

The churchyard figures frequently in his notes, leaving a picture worth recording. He commonly let the grazing in the churchyard with sometimes unexpected results. As he says in a letter to Mr Reed of the See Ho, one of his churchwardens:

> 'Witness the great complaints yt have been made all the last winter long and a considerable time before of the churchyard being so often stocked with hogs. And as they are said to belong mostly to one of the churchwardens it makes the case so much the more scandalous.'

Hogs were not the only trouble in the churchyard. As Mr Parfect notes – and his notes are more descriptive than any historian's solemn recording – 'The people yt belong to the neighbouring gardens should be desired not to throw their weeds and trumpery into the churchyard as a place very improper for dunghills to be made in.' The practice seems to have created a great heap of rubbish near to the belfry and around the yew trees, which Mr Parfect remarks were 'planted by our forefathers' so they were obviously old in his day.[1] After some correspondence he managed to get his churchwarden Mr Reed to cart some of the rubbish away in a broadwheeled cart.

As a contrast Mr Parfect did what he could to improve the appearance of the churchyard. In 1765 he notes that he had planted eight chestnut trees observing 'vistas and trees are much used to set off gentlemen's houses and why should they not be made to grace in the best manner possible the way that goes up to the house of God'. Most of these trees survived until some fifteen years ago, but three only remain today.

Mr Parfect's interest in the morals and behaviour of his parishioners gives us many unexpected and notable period pictures of Shorne in the eighteenth century. The public house, the Billett, was directly opposite the vicarage, but Mr Parfect was no teetotaller, and took no notice of the somewhat casual establishment of the inn mentioned in an earlier chapter, until Mr French gave up his licence. Then for a moment another character and custom appear briefly in this history. A bricklayer in the village named Little, needing a wife, looked around and found one who was for sale, named Benning. He came to an arrangement with her husband (Mr Parfect says a document was signed and sealed, but does not record the price) and the lady was sold to Mr Little, taking over the duties of Mrs Little. The village was scandalised, but could do little about it until the Billett became vacant, when Little 'and his bargain' as Mr Parfect happily describes her, proposed to take the licence. Mr Parfect at once started a correspondence with the licensing bench, and the whole scandal is recited in letters which he copied into his tithe book, with a final note 'the method I made use of to defeat this scandalous project proved successful.'

The morals of another villager also engaged the vicar's attention. This man seems to have made a practice of rearing families by his housemaids. The first had two children by him, but was got away and married off. When the whole process began again with another maid, Mr Parfect moved into action. He bullied his churchwardens into presenting the second girl before the archdeacon for immorality — an ancient practice long obsolete — to the archdeacon's dismay. Correspondence with the archdeacon followed, but in the middle of the argument, the man put up the bans and married the woman, to Mr Parfect's delight. The last line of his notes on the subject are 'which gives particular pleasure to etc etc C.P.'

Quite a different type of offence is illustrated in another of his many notes. In 1764 on Sunday 23rd September, Mr Parfect, coming out of church after service, found two or three men with a long ladder and 'on enquiring what the occasion of so extraordinary a phenominum might be' he discovered that they were men employed by a plumber of Milton next Gravesend named Mears, sent by him to do some work on the roof of the church. He seems to have said little to the men, who were only carrying out their orders, but sent at once to Mr Curry, curate of Milton, to ask him to 'chastise him for it', and a day or so later he himself met Mr Mears when 'I took proper notice of his impudence and moreover told him he had forfeited 5/- for using his trade on the Lord's day'. Mr Mears was apparently overwhelmed and sent the five shillings to Mr Nun, the churchwarden of Shorne, who at the vicar's request gave two shillings to Mrs Bellamore, two shillings to Widow Caryer, and one shilling to Widow Pummice.

The arrangement of church services is revealed by Mr Parfect's notes. The order of bell ringing before Sunday services is set out two or three times in the parish books. The first bell was at seven o'clock, the second at eight, and the sermon bell at nine. Then it was chimed three times at ten, and again at a quarter after, before tolling into the church at half an hour after ten. The afternoon bell in the summer followed the same sequence. First bell at twelve, second at one, and a sermon bell at two o'clock with tolling in at three, but in the winter the service began at quarter past two. 'Not a bell to *stir* at *any other time*' he adds. Obviously he was no lover of bell ringing.

The services themselves were no doubt the broadest of Church of England broad church. We learn however that towards the end of his incumbency he accepted that the services should be enhanced by singing, and a fund was set up to employ a master to instruct young people in the singing of the psalms, though 'Playford's and no other' tunes were to be sung. Playford's tunes were first published some hundred years before, so the vicar can hardly be deemed revolutionary in his tastes.

He notes several rearrangements of pews, and records that the women and girls of the lower orders were segregated in a special pew. Likewise he observes that the font formerly (apparently before his time), stood against the left-hand pillar of the middle arch of the arcade between the nave and the south aisle.

Mr Parfect was constantly preoccupied with the repair and improvement of the vicarage. The work varied from rebuilding the old main chimney stack, to wainscoting the parlour. He and his wife and family never missed a summer there, but though he seems to have loved the old house, spending much time and money on it, he groans in one entry:

'Beware of an old house as attended with an endless expense.'

A thought which many owners of old houses have repeated over the centuries.

During those years his family was growing up, and his daughter Elizabeth seems to have attracted the attention of John Tomlin, one of the tanner's family, at that time the licensee of the White Horse. He was a widower and a substantial villager when on 13th December 1743 he married Elizabeth. Tragedy followed, for on 2nd July the following year John Tomlin died, 'cut off in his strength by the small pox' as his gravestone by the church door still records. On 20th September John, the posthumous child of John Tomlin, was born, and the child's burial a month later is recorded by the grandfather in the registers without comment.

It seems that Mr Parfect was known to have a soft heart for people who took their responsibilities seriously. In February 1759 Thomas and Elizabeth Higgins of Cobham made all the arrangements for their child William to be baptised, but as Mr Parfect notes:

'Mr Chapman being ill and no service at Cobham yt day the child was brought from Cobham to Shorne to be baptised, a favour not well to be refused the people being poor and had preparation for the christening.'

During winter time Mr Parfect was not resident at Shorne, but the Higgins family must have relied on him being at Shorne for a service, before they started off on their long trudge to Shorne church. Similarly in 1763, this time in April,

John and Ann Cook, living at Three Crutches, carried their child to Cobham in the morning to be baptised, but arrived too late, and being very disappointed, carried it to Shorne in the afternoon and 'at the pressing instance of Cook himself and his father-in-law Johnson' Mr Parfect baptised the child though not of his parish.

Some traces of village festive occasions are recorded in Mr Parfect's notes. The annual beating of the bounds was of course an ancient custom and Mr Parfect in his tithe book gives an elaborate diagram all round the edges of two pages of the book, setting out the bounds marks, none of which can now be identified because practically all of them were trees, of one species or another, now long lost. The poor rate books occasionally record expenses for beating the bounds, and the vicars' letters on more than one occasion make it clear that the bounds were beaten on Ascension day, and that the major part of the parish took part. We may imagine a large party trudging the lengthy bounds, having much drinking and merriment on the way, ending with a bounds feast.

One event in which Mr Parfect was personally concerned was the annual tithe feast, showing, from his remarks, that all his troubles over tithes were forgotten at least once a year. A picture of this eighteenth century vicar remains when in his old age writing to Mr Gordon he remarks:

> 'were you incog. at a tithe feast you would be hugely surprised and much concerned to see the many difficulties we are ever engaging with . . . The shrewdness of the farmer yt so invariably runs thro' every article of business wch comes into question is amazing – and what vicar without a pocket (wch he seldom has) can never be a proper match for . . . Old age keeps me under and perfectly tractable. Wranglings are tiresome and I had rather sit and hear the debates de re rustica wch generally arise as such parish meetings.'

So we can see the old man after a lifetime of parochial activity sitting amongst his parishioners, enjoying their talk and looking back over some thirty-five years of faithful service to the community. Perhaps the most satisfactory of his recollections was a matter which justifies a separate chapter – his re-establishment of the Lady Page charity after a long quarrel with Mr Maplesden and the parish officers.

1. Two ancient yew trees still stand in the north east and north west corners of the churchyard. If the commonly accepted longevity of yew trees is correct these may well have been trees planted to mark the boundaries of the 'sacred acre' when Christianity first came to Shorne.

Pound Cottage, or Miss Bird's cottage. The village pound stood to the west of the cottage and was a small spike-fenced enclosure at one time used to store the parish fire engine. Miss Bird was a village schoolmistress who lived in the cottage for many years. Council development now occupies the site.

The site of Pound Cottage today.

## Chapter 14
## THE PRESERVATION OF CHARITY

It will be remembered that the Lady Page Charity was finally established after delays of nearly fifty years. By the beginning of the eighteenth century the rent of the field purchased with her legacy was being applied in accordance with the terms of her will. In 1712 John Massey was bound to George Nash, a tailor of Gravesend, with a premium of £10 (a high premium for those days) provided by the charity, and in 1716 the surviving trustees took care to appoint new trustees.

At this point however there was a change in the administration of the charity. Two years after the new trustees were appointed, entries in the Overseers' accounts show that the rent of the field was being paid directly into the overseers' hands, and they seem to have paid for such matters as the letting of the field, repairing the gates, and paying the manorial quit rent. The money simply went to relieve the rates and there is no record of any children being apprenticed.

Even in the eighteenth century this could not go on for long, and towards the end of the 1720s another practice was adopted. The tenant of the field (who was generally a vestryman if not a parish officer) was allowed to retain the rent in his own pocket until such time as the overseers found a child in the village they wanted to apprentice. They then asked the tenant for the premium which he paid out of the rents he owed. Thus the years passed. The trustees, quite indifferent, died off one by one and after a generation or so it is likely that the field would have been treated as the property of the tenant, and the trust would have disappeared, had not someone come forward to halt the process.

Mr Parfect in the early days of his ministry at Shorne seems to have thought little about the charity, but in 1747 Mr Cadwell the tenant of the field died, and his executor was Jarvis Maplesden. It is possible that this change in the tenancy of the field first brought the matter to Mr Parfect's notice, though he seems to have proceeded with caution.

Four years after Mr Cadwell's death he noted in his records the opening shots of what was to prove a long war with the parish officers and the tenant of the field. On Easter Monday 1751, Jarvis Maplesden, William Tomlin, H. Gooden, Thos. Downing, Steven Overy, and Richard Caryer attended the usual vestry to approve accounts, appoint churchwardens and nominate overseers – also to have a good time at the expense of the poor rate, the customary refreshments on this occasion amount to £1.4s.3d., a fair sum with liquor prices at 2d. to 4d. a quart. For once the even calm of a routine meeting was disturbed by Mr Parfect, and the incident cannot be better recorded than in his own words in the note he made in the registers.

'On Easter Monday 1751 at a vestry appointed for choosing parish officers the vicar earnestly pressed the necessity of keeping Lady Page's charity on the footing so fully intended by her will which Mr J.M. (churchwarden) violently opposed and tho' no tolerable reason was nor could be given for his doing so (unless the charitys being made to ease the common rates and to serve no other use can be reckn'd one) . . . '

The note goes on at length, and on the next page of the registers is another long note on charities of which the following extract will give some idea of the way in which Mr Parfect's mind was working:

'Alms are a *sacred thing* . . . to divert them from the end intended . . . *sacrilege* . . . not to *give* alms is sin that merits damnation but to steal . . . is monstrous iniquity – this was the crime of Judas . . .'

After an outburst like this it is somewhat surprising to find that the matter seems to have been allowed to fall into oblivion – at least so far as our records reveal. There were difficulties. By this time all the trustees appointed in 1716 were dead, likewise it was difficult to find out what had happened to the rents of the field, and it was not until 1762, over ten years later, that the heir of William Cottman, the last surviving trustee, was traced, and persuaded to appoint new trustees.

The new trustees were an impressive array. The Earl of Darnley, Francis Barrett, William Gordon (Lord of the manor), Jarvis Maplesden, the Revd Thomas Buttenshaw (vicar of Addington and Ryarsh), the Revd Parfect, George Holmes and James Cadwell. Again there was a lull in the affairs of the charity until 1765/6. As Mr Parfect says in another note, it was difficult to procure 'such a state of the charity . . . as was fit . . . to be presented to the feoffees'. During the lull however Mr Parfect found two allies, both typical of the age. The first was Mr Gordon, Lord of the Manor, with whom he had been on friendly terms for many years. Here was the status needed to offset the Maplesden influence in the village, against which the next step would have to be taken. To this end he was appointed Receiver of the charity. The second ally was the redoubtable Mr Twopenny, attorney-at-law, also of Rochester, a member of a firm whose name survived locally into living memory (an ancient threat in neighbours' quarrels was 'I'll take you to Twopennys'). He handled the complicated legal technicalities.

The rent situation was confused. James Cadwell, the former tenant, had died in 1747, and Mr Maplesden as his executor had taken over and been in occupation of the field ever since, whether as executor or nominal tenant was not clear. No one knew when the last rent had been paid by Mr Cadwell, and by the time Mr Twopenny took the matter up it seems that Mr Maplesden had begun to consider himself the owner of the field.

All the correspondence was preserved by Mr Parfect in a carefully written minute book. Mr Twopenny's first letter requesting an account was ignored, and further letters from the lawyer followed until in March 1767 Mr Maplesden seems to have realised he would have to deal with the matter as a simple claim for arrears of rent, and condescended to leave at Mr Twopenny's office an account which reveals a curious situation. The statement reads:

'Mr J. Maplesden commenced tenant for the parish field
   at Shorne Michs 1746 at 40/- per ann to Do 1766 18 years    £36. 0. 0.
   Paid in part to Mr Thomas Tomlin overseer of the said parish    8. 0. 0.
                                                                                                                       28. 0. 0.
Paid more by 3 years rent of the house that the parish had of
   me at £3 p.a.    9. 0. 0.
                                                                                                            19. 0. 0.
Paid more for many years quit rent paid and to pay
Paid do. for repairs to the barrs during that time    1.10. 0.
Paid more by landtax not settled on that being so long used
   by the farmer charged all in one'

Mr Twopenny's reply dissected this statement in detail. He required Mr Maplesden to account for the rent of Mr Cadwell's tenancy, which he suggested added another nine years to the total rent to be accounted for. 'An amazing term' he observes. Mr Maplesden's cottage was used by the overseers to house the poor and was a charge on the rates, not the charity. The claim that moneys had been paid to the overseer Thomas Tomlin besides being unsupported by any voucher or receipt, was not only a wrong payment of the money, but also a payment to 'a man who happened not to have the fairest character in the parish nor the world' — an odd comment about a parishioner who must have been related to Parfect's former son-in-law.

These objections stung Mr Maplesden into a formal reply alleging the custom of the parish was to leave the rents in the hands of the tenant (whom he said the parish believed to be trusted) until a sufficient sum had accrued to apprentice children. He also produced details of earlier payments to the overseers:

'During the time I was in trust for James Cadwell ... the parish called on me for the sum of
30th March 1750    £7.10. 0.
March 1    6.10. 0.
and May 4    9. 0. 0.
One pound of which last payment they told me was due from Mr Cadwell and the other £8 was on my own account.'

After this Mr Twopenny wrote that he would call 'this day sennight' in the morning for a settlement. He appears to have called at Pipes Place and had a frosty reception. Mr Maplesden refused to go back to Mr Cadwell's arrears, and finally Mr Twopenny accepted £28 in settlement.

The curious thing about this quarrel is that Mr Maplesden's sixteen-year-old recollections of payments to the dubious Mr Tomlin were correct. In the parish chest are three apprenticeship deeds dated March 1st 1750, 5th April 1751, and

3rd May 1751 which show that Mr Maplesden had in fact paid the three amounts set out in his statement. True the children were only apprenticed to learn 'husbandry' and 'housewifery', and Mr Tomlin may have had a rake-off, but Mr Maplesden could have silenced the lawyer's (and vicar's) innuendoes about his accounting had he cared to look in the parish chest.

The recovery of the money belonging to the charity was of course but a step. The next step, to restrain the parish officers from simply using the money to relieve the rates, was equally difficult. Mr Parfect always contended that the apprenticeships were not intended to provide premiums to put out parish paupers, but rather the children of poor but respectable villagers. This the overseers were most reluctant to accept. Mr Parfect wrote to Mr Gordon, the Receiver, on the matter and his letter sets out his views in his inimitable way and is worth quoting as a guide to the general attitude of parish officers in those days.

> 'Good sir, (he writes), I was not yet from dinner wh your kind answer came ... vext yt any misrepresentation. Lady Pages charity has most certainly been very much abused (and few escape being so). It has principally serv'd to get parish orphans *out* of the parish and too often put to poor people ... and *who* can be supposed to leave charities for *such* and *the like purposes*? This lady's will is plainly guarded against such malepractices; tho' we have too much proof yt 'tis extremely difficult to prevent them — and when *parish officers* come to lay hold of such bequests they seldom scruple to convert 'em to *any* purpose yt may save *their own* pockets ...'

Whilst the Lady Page charity troubles were in full spate the vicar found time to turn his attention to another charity incident typical of the age. Dr Ayerst had recently died and left a legacy to be distributed amongst the poor. The parish officers had apparently suggested that it might well be distributed at Mr Reed's 'See Ho' public house. Mr Parfect wrote at once to Mr Reed urging him to distribute the Ayerst legacy with the annual Peters Pence distribution at the church door on St Peter's day, suggesting how a substantial sum which the Ayerst legacy would provide might be used by the poor 'a parcel of linen etc much wanted' 'a poor family may be set at liberty and clear'd of a vexatious long standing debt' and so on. After his copy of this letter in his tithe accounts he adds one or two pointed comments:

> 'The money ... was brought — the poor much pleased and thankful and the *people* greatly disappointed that intended a *slight* to the minister on that occasion.'

> 'Some drunken *folks must* share in the charity thro' Reeds civility to them and his own interest as a publican.'

A quiet postscript to the whole Lady Page charity dispute at this point came when after the death of Mr Maplesden (he never gave up the field) the question of re-letting it arose, and Mr Parfect wrote once again to Mr Twopenny in May 1769 with his views on re-letting:

'Sir, I am ashamed to trouble you so often . . . about the letting of the field whether it might not be proper to try at it next Ascension day when we purpose to go the parish bounds and the major part of the parish will be together.'

He then suggests that with a view to selecting one or two apprentices he invite Mr Gordon the Receiver to dine with them at the house when 'our bounds feast will be ready'. He then goes on:

'His tenant Noakes I understand is to get the poor children of the parish together to be seen by Mr Gordon, but . . . needless trouble. A list of them (only little chaps most of ym I daresay fit for *cow boys* etc and what the farmers ought to take themselves) will do . . . I am willing to lend my assistance . . . it may be of some service to what may soon be passed elsewhere by

Yr most humble servant C. Parfect.'

It is a pity that all we now know about these plans is that Mrs Maplesden continued as tenant of the field for some years and that at this point we take our farewell of the indomitable old parson, who, having outlived his opponent Mr Maplesden, passed to his anticipated rest a few months later, to be buried at Cuxton.

Swillers Lane. The building on the left was the village slaughter-house which formerly stood to the south of the church, but which was rebuilt in this position by the late G.M. Arnold.

Swillers Lane today.

## Chapter 15
## THE POOR HOUSE

Until the middle of the eighteenth century, the normal number of villagers regularly relieved in a year was between four and six, and the annual rate charged on the ratepayers was around sixty pounds a year. From 1758 however there was a rapid increase in the total annual rate levied and in the number of those relieved. By 1760 there were nineteen poor relieved to a greater or lesser degree and there were three assessments of a shilling in the pound during that year, producing a total of £245 to meet the disbursements. Some idea of the growth of the work of the overseers can be gained from the fact that there are fifty four pages of accounts for the whole year.

This growth also led to a rapid change in the outlook of the overseers which, though at first tempered by the earlier tradition, gradually adopted the 'workhouse' philosophy of the nineteenth century.

It seems that the idea of some sort of communal housing of the poor was under discussion. In November 1761 the vestry met 'pursuant to a public notice' in the parish church and adjourned to the White Horse, where it was agreed that jointly with the parish of Chalk an agreement should be entered into with one Giles Scotford of Northfleet 'for the maintenance educating clothing and provision for the poor of the said parishes respectively and to hire a poor house for that purpose'. Nothing further seems to have been done about this scheme, the old system of weekly payments and general relief continuing as before until 1767.

The first half of that year seems similar in every way to the preceding years, but in the second half we find a poor house in full operation, without any clear evidence of how it came about.

It seems that Dame Patience ('Pashins' as William Bilboe the overseer called her) who had received rate assistance fell into arrear with her rent and her goods were distrained by Mr Fenner, her landlord. The parish paid him two pounds for these goods and removed them to the 'poor house' with Dame Patience as part of the chattels. Then in the second half of the year, instead of sixteen people drawing weekly relief, there are only six (two of them in Cobham College) and two children being 'kept' whilst in lieu of weekly payments we find monthly payments of between four and five pounds 'for the keep of the por of the hous'. This is supplemented by 'Beer for the por' and a chaldron of coals 'for the house'. A little later there is the payment of ten shillings and six pence for 'yarn for the yous of the hous'.

The location of the poor house is not indicated, but tradition in the village says it was the house, now demolished, which had the yew tree in its front garden. This tree now stands in the middle of the road at the bottom of Tanyard Hill.

The later accounts for 1797 contain a list of furniture in the 'house' which not only gives some idea of the accommodation available for the poor, but also what was available by way of furniture for their comfort.

| | |
|---|---|
| 'In the parlour | One oake leaf table. |
| In the pantry | One deal table, 1 chest, one powdering tub, six baking dishes, 6 plates, 6 breakfast pans, 8 trenchers. |
| In kitchen | 8 chairs, 3 tables, 2 forms, warming pan, 5 iron candlesticks, grates as fixt, 1 pr of pot hooks. |
| Cellar | 2 iron bound casks, 4 wash keelers, baking tub, mash tub, 2 halders, 2 pails, 3 iron pots. |
| In washhouse | One copper and large iron pot as fixt. |
| Chamber over the kitchen | 3 beds, 3 bedsteads, 1 pr drawers, 3 chests, 6 pr new sheets, 10 pr old sheets, 6 new blanketts, 9 old blankets, 4 new coverlidds, 6 old coverlidds. |
| Chamber over parlour | 2 bedsteads with hangings and one bedstead without, 3 beds, 3 chairs and 2 chests. |
| In attic storey | 2 bedsteads, 2 beds, 1 chest, 1 sidebed.' |

We know that twenty years before Dame Patience's goods had formed the beginning of this furnishing, and apart from soft furnishings such as sheets, towels, table-cloths, and the like little else seems to have been purchased by the overseers, so we must assume the bulk of the furnishing was acquired by taking over the furniture of those taken into the house.

The food provided for those in the house can be judged from the various bills paid. In the three months of January, February and March in 1774 there were, according to a sort of diary kept in the account book by the overseers, seven adults and five children in the house. In February Mr Cable the butcher was paid 11s.3d. for 'five stone of beef at 2/3'. In March he was paid for a bullock's head costing 2s.6d. as well as for another five stone of beef at 2s.3d. On 12th March 4 stone 9lb of beef and a week later another 4 stone 7lb of beef went into the house. In March one and a half chaldrons of coal were paid for, and on April 1st Mr Bilboe the miller had £11 for his bill covering a period from November. Mr Nunn's bill for small beer came to £1 and Mr Noakes' account for milk was five shillings. Mr Noakes also provided five bushels of potatoes at 4s.6d. Bacon sometimes supplemented the beef, and on one occasion ten pecks of beans were purchased. Butter and cheese are more rarely mentioned, though we have no means of determining what was provided for in the undetailed 'bills' paid to individuals whose trade we do not know.

All these items suggest rough, monotonous but plentiful food and with the furniture, and the coal, life in the 'house' was not bad for its inmates. Indeed when we find an item 'Paid Rogers on his promising to keep out of the house 2/-' it seems the house had its attractions to some.

For a while the poor house was used as a place from which the poor were expected to go out to work for the benefit of the parish. The idea of putting the poor to work was an old one, but there is little trace of this in the earlier accounts. On two occasions in the early eighteenth century a spinning wheel was purchased for the poor, but if the wheel was used the rates did not benefit, unless the occasional references in the accounts for money received for the 'goods of the poor' is not for the sale of paupers' furniture, but for spun yarn.

The first clear indication that the poor were expected to work to relieve the rates are a number of small payments from one Dame Purnice and later from Dame Patience who seem to have been overseers or supervisors of the poor. Details of the early payments are not given, but in 1768 after the establishment of the poor house the entries become more explicit:

| 'June 28th | Received of Mr Packham for Dame Pelham nursing his maid | 6. 0d. |
|---|---|---|
| 28th | Received ditto for Ellen Turner picking turnips | 6. 0d. |
| Sept 10th | Earnt picking of hops in my ground by the poor | 1. 8. 0d. |
| Oct 25th | Recd for picking hops by the poor in Mr Gordon's ground | 12. 0d. |
| | Recd of Mr Grayham for stone picking done by the poor | 9. 2d.' |

The experiment did not last for long however and by the mid 1770s it was quietly dropped and not repeated.

The increases in the number of the poor and the cost of maintaining them led to changes in administration. In the 1780s it seems to have become customary for each overseer to be responsible for a separate half year and to render his accounts for that half year only. This necessitated more frequent vestries. The old 'charge' by the magistrates in 1597 had required the overseers to meet monthly, but there is little trace of this in the earlier accounts. By the end of the eighteenth century however there are indications in the accounts that monthly meetings were then being held, and this is confirmed by a curious 'agreement' which survives amongst the routine accounts.

As early as 1703 odd entries occur in the accounts like one by Thomas Ratley:

'Spent when I recd ye money of ye old overseer several of
ye parishioners being present                                              2. 8d.'

As the century passed it seems to have become customary for refreshment to be provided at vestry and other parish meetings at the expense of the rates. In 1708 it cost 9s.1d. when the parish met 'two times', and the amount increased steadily over the years. No doubt the news got around, and those entitled to attend the vestry took advantage of this chance of free refreshment. In the thirties the annual vestries seem normally to have been held at the White Horse and the expenses grew to an average of about fourteen shillings a meeting, whilst the numbers attending the vestry also increased.

No doubt the idea was popular with the licensees as well as the vestrymen, and as the complexity of administration grew towards the end of the eighteenth century, and the 'expenses' mounted, the licensees of the village all wanted an equal share of this steady and profitable trade. So in 1780 an agreement was drawn up whereby the overseers and parishioners agreed:

> 'To meet at the several public houses in the parish of Shorne the last Monday in the month (each public house taking it by regular turns monthly) to meet by 5 o'clock in the evening then and there to inspect ye poor's accounts every vestryman here signing not attending at the time appointed to forfeit sixpence, if either of the officers not attending at the time appointed to forfeit one shilling and if the poor book is not brought for inspection then in that case the two officers to forfeit half a crown.'

Some twenty names are appended though they appear to have been altered, added to, or deleted from time to time after the original signing. By this orderly arrangement the licensees could expect between ten and fifteen shillings' worth of trade every month at one or other house and the annual vestry meeting, a more important affair, seems to have sometimes had over three pounds in expenses.

The events of the 1770s and 1780s were soon to be clouded with the wars of the end of the century, which had an effect on parish life needing an entirely separate chapter, though many of the details are culled from the poor law books covering that period.

## Chapter 16
## WAR AND PEACE

The wars of the eighteenth century leave little trace in our records. In Mr Parfect's time one Eades was 'pressed for a soldier' leaving his wife and two children on the parish, and a lengthy case to counsel about the parish liability to maintain the children gives a lot of information about his family affairs — his wife had married below her and her father had disowned her — but we do not know where he went with the army. Again a little later there is another reference to 'taking up' William Richardson and sending him for a soldier, but these matters seem to have caused little stir in village life.

The wars generally called the Napoleonic wars, however, were very different. The first impact of the war with France on the enclosed village life was the construction of Shornemead Fort on the riverside edge of the ancient common marsh of the manor. The fort was finished in 1795/6 and the village must have thought war was really coming their way when cannon were mounted there, and the old manor way and drove roads across the common marsh became the access to the fort.

In January 1797 the pressure of war on village finances became more apparent. The year begins with a curious entry in the accounts:

'Parish of Shorne part for raising the sailors for the navy
as settled at Mr Monks Cobham                £28. 16. 2½d.'

In the same month the overseers were called before the justices concerning the militia, whilst in February three soldiers' wives with children passing through the village were relieved by a payment of two shillings and six pence.

The mutiny at the Nore is faintly reflected in the overseers' accounts. The mutinous ships could easily be seen from the hill at Shorne as they lay moored in two lines in Sea Reach. Cruden, the Gravesend historian, gives much information about the events locally, including the manning of the riverside forts at Shorne Mead, Gravesend and Tilbury, though he does not mention that the local militia was embodied. The parish records make it clear that these local men were called up temporarily. The overseers were summonsed again to Rochester in May 'concerning the pay of the supplementary militia' and a week or so later Cable of Shorne was paid one week's pay for the militia at four shillings.

According to Cruden when a boat containing a delegation from the fleet was approaching the landing stage at Shornemead Fort one of the fort's twelve-pounders fired a shot, and we can well imagine the villagers were startled. However the final ending of the mutiny in June with its delegates and negotiations at Sheerness moved the focus of these troubles well outside the Shorne area.

After this the long wars are reflected year by year in the overseers' accounts as the requirements of the militia affected villagers. If a man was balloted for either the militia or the regular army, his wife and children were almost certain to come on the rates. It was therefore well worth while for the overseers to join with the unlucky man in finding a substitute who had no wife or children. This not only led to curiously muddled arrangements, but enables us to follow the impact of the war on the villagers.

Sometimes the substitute seems to have been paid a lump sum of about £12.10s.0d., and sometimes he was paid a weekly sum. Probably the lump sum payment was to a man who went into the regular army, and the weekly payment to a man called into the militia. The pace increased after the war was resumed in 1803 and there are several entries about substitutes in that year. One concerned John Campbell who was paid £12.10s.0d. 'for being drough for the army of Reserve': another payment was £6.10s.0d. for a substitute for William Merchant, where presumably William Merchant paid the rest himself. A variation was the payment of 8s.0d. per week for James Weeks, serving as a substitute for 51 weeks, which cost the parish £20.14s.0d., which illustrates why a lump sum was preferred.

The following year, with the Napoleonic Army on the other side of the Channel, and invasion expected, brought even more work for the overseers and the militia. Substitutes of all sorts were provided. Amongst them we find £12.10s.0d. paid to Mr Cannon for a substitute for his son George. Mr Cannon was at this time the tenant farmer of Cheneys Farm, Thong, and the licensee of the Yorkshire Gray public house at Thong, and one wonders why he could not pay the amount himself. Another payment was of £10 to 'James Taylor by an order deemed unfit for service'. One must wonder what was behind this payment, which looks like a Social Benefit payment rather than the crude poor law economics of the period.

The clearest indication of the invasion scare is when the wives and children of five villagers were all relieved for two weeks in 1804, the men being described as 'on actual duty for a fortnight'. In 1805 there is an unusual item of:

'13 May Pd for five men difficient in militia and army of reserve £100.0s.0d.'

This large sum was repaid by the Receiver General in the following year without further explanation.

In 1806 the overseers were preparing a militia schedule and delivering it upon oath at a cost of £1.10s.6d., a minor chore to add to their other duties which continued annually until some years after the war was over. By this time there seems to have been a sort of accepted reservoir of 'cannon fodder' who seem to have made a regular occupation of providing militia substitutes. For instance James Weeks appears three times in the accounts over the years as a substitute, until in 1808 he was actually called up. What lay behind this complicated affair is not clear. As the years passed the price of a substitute increased to £15.

The beginning of the Peninsular campaigns leaves a record in the accounts with an entry in 1808:

> 'Paid Mrs Pugh 2 weeks pay as by agreement of vestry her husband embarked for Spain                8. 0d.'

In 1809 overseers attended a local militia meeting with three volunteers, and later meetings of a similar description year by year suggest the overseers acted almost as recruiting officers. It is worth recording that six of the named men in the Napoleonic war militia bore the same names as men who served in the Shorne Home Guard in 1940-1944.

Apart from the continuous passing of formed bodies of troops along the Dover Road, the poor or injured soldier or sailor was a regular reminder of the war, but as the years passed the passage of the wives of soldiers and their children became a notable feature. Three sailors' wives with children in 1804 were a warning of things to come, and from 1807 onwards there was a great flood of them on the highway. On 3rd March the parish relieved six passes with 285 women and children at £2.17s.6d. On 8th and 9th of the same month another five passes with 292 soldiers' wives and children 'from abroad' passed by and were relieved. On the 11th yet another 410 wives and children were followed on the 14th by 596 wives and children and on the 21st by 508. In one month over two thousand of this debris of war passed through the village. It is difficult to determine which particular campaign caused this flood; probably the last attempt of Pitt to land forces in Europe in the latter part of 1805. Such a mass of people passing through must have filled all the barns and outbuildings in the village.

With the Peninsular War the origin of these travellers is recorded. After small numbers in 1809 in January 1810 comes the significant entry:

> 'Relieved 4 passes wt 296 soldiers' wives and children from Corruna etc                £2.5s.0d.'

Much has been written about the hardships of that retreat across Spain, and here are some of the women and children who had been in the battered army which had embarked at Corunna, back to England at last, receiving beggars' relief as they made their way, who knows whither?

The story repeats itself in 1812 and 1813 with wives and children from Spain and Portugal.

Then in 1814 the long drawn out struggle ended with a different traveller on the highway, when the bellringers of Shorne were paid £2 for ringing the bells as the King of France passed along the Dover Road on his way to his kingdom.

The village then had to grapple with the aftermath. In the twenty years of war the old unchanging customs, the hierarchy of squire, yeoman and villager from the relatively wealthy farmer or tradesman to the almost hereditary pauper, which had preserved a balance of society throughout the preceding centuries, underwent a complete change, and it was at the extremities of squire and pauper that the changes were most marked. We will relate the changes of landownership in the next chapter, but the story of the poorer element in the village forms a fitting epilogue to the chapter on war.

The relief of the poor had, by the end of the war, become an overwhelming problem. The poor rate averaged between six and seven hundred pounds a year, and though the expenses of the militia had ended, in the post-war years it continued to rise until it was normally over a thousand pounds a year. Behind the rise in the rates was a rising population, whilst inflation caused the old relief of two or three shillings a week to be increased to upwards of ten shillings a week.

Some indication of the pressure on the overseers was the introduction of an annual payment by way of salary. In 1808 it was £10 a year, but this was increased to £20 in the following years. Similarly instead of the casual medical attendance upon the sick we find Dr Jones retained at an annual fee plus special fees on special occasions.

There was a distinctly war and post-war atmosphere about the moral outlook of villagers as revealed in the rate accounts. In the seventeenth and eighteenth centuries bastardy is rarely mentioned, perhaps one case coming to the overseers every twenty or thirty years. During the war and post-war periods there is a marked change. In 1797 for instance there were four bastardy cases taking up the overseers' time, and by the middle of the war period and thereafter, a year seldom passes without a case of a girl 'swearing her child'. The father, if traced, normally paid an agreed sum either in one amount or by instalments to the overseers who then made weekly payments to the mother. One or two cases make quite dramatic reading in the 'penny novelette' style which we have found on other village occasions.

For instance, an entry on August 30th 1816 reads:

'Attending Susan Pattison to swear her son to
Sir John Richardson                                             2. 6d.'

On September 2nd the accounts record:

'Attending with Susan Pattison                                  3. 6d.
'Paid for coroners warrant to search Chalk churchyard
for Susan Pattisons infant (& found it there) & expenses        6. 0d.'

Further entries mark the end of the story. 'Attending jury at Chalk', 'Attending second jury at Chalk', 'Attending third examination of S. Pattison'. The child being dead we hear no more about Sir John.

Not infrequently the 'swearing' was followed by a 'Knobstick' wedding as on the occasion in 1821 when two villagers were married with a gift from the rates of £3, parson's and clerk's fees of 10s.6d. and refreshments provided at the cost of 3s.6d. by the rates.

Bastardy was not the only indication of a changing parish ethos. In 1815 the accounts have a note:

'W. Chittenden and W. Hornsblow sent to Maidstone for sheep steeling.
Wm Sutton turned King's evidence'
'Do. got bail and went home 12th May'

There are many entries for the overseers' time attending sessions when villagers were before the courts, clearly nothing to do with arrears of rates or matters of that sort, and occasionally a note records that the prisoner was sent to jail. Likewise the borseholder had regular 'bills' for amounts of up to £4 in a year, besides odd items of the old sort for carrying 'vagrants' to the 'Cage' at Strood, sometimes by the cartload.

It seems likely that the 'bills' conceal a deterioration in standards which is revealed by a block of entries in 1820:

| | |
|---|---|
| 'Cashfield for taken Daniel Down and flogging May 4 | 10. 0d. |
| Thomas Cross laying about & being flogged June 9th | 10. 0d. |
| John May taken in Court Wood and flogged 21st | 10. 0d. |
| Thos Peel given themselves up being July 12 and | |
| Thomas Stevens the same flogged Aug 10 | 1. 0. 0d. |
| Richard Clark taken and flogged May 16 | 10. 0d.' |

Two centuries before there are records of the whipping post at the churchyard gates, but no record of its use occurs in all our voluminous records until this occasion. The entries are not repeated, but the use of the word 'flogged' instead of the older term 'whipped' suggests a changed attitude to corporal punishment in this period.

By the end of the war the old poor house was insufficient to house the increasing number of paupers, and the overseers were once again renting cottages to house the homeless poor. Some of the entries in the accounts show that the old idea of sharing accommodation with Chalk had been revived as certain items of poor house expenses are marked in the accounts 'shared between Chalk and Shorne', though the exact arrangement is not recorded.

By 1818 these arrangements were quite inadequate. Two ideas were put in hand, the building of a new workhouse, and the use of the old Shorne Mead Fort buildings on the riverside marshes, abandoned by the army after the war. The two schemes seem to have been put into use at the same time. Whilst the new workhouse was being built, the overseers patched up the windows and gutters of the fort, and for several years thereafter, even after the new poor house had been built, some of the poor were housed in that remote, damp and unhealthy place, its gloom only relieved by occasional loads of coal.

Without the Revd Parfect being there to raise objections to the old idea of using a charity to help the rates, the overseers took over the Lady Page Charity field, and built the workhouse thereon with the assistance of an annuity purchased by Mr Costello for £400. The workhouse still stands as a private house on the Dover Road, and in it are the cellars in which prisoners were placed, chains for this purpose being purchased by the overseers. Even today the house stands alone and isolated from the village, and one senses in the remoteness a change in sentiment from the centre of the community outlook of the site of the older poor house. For some three or four years the overseers paid no rent for the field, but in 1824 Mr Staines the vicar was being paid 'rent for the poor house field' at twelve pounds a year.

The old village poor house had been run by the 'Mistress', Mrs Cashfield, and when the new workhouse was completed the overseers appointed Mr Cashfield, the flogging borseholder, and his wife as joint workhouse masters. They undertook the maintenance of the poor in the house at so much per head. From the bare entries in the accounts one gets the impression that it was very differently run from the old easy-going days of 'Dame Patience' with the idle coming and going of the poor and payments to some to keep out of the house. Cashfield the master is perhaps best summed up by the occasion of his departure, when he was discharged 'For being continuously in a state of beastly intoxication'. One wonders what life in the 'house' was like under his rule.

The old world of the Elizabethan poor law was about to end, and a few years later came the Poor Law Act of 1835, under which the unions were formed and the poor moved to the Union Workhouse at Strood. The rate book for the last few years of the overseers' administration is missing, so we have no final details of the passing of this so intimate part of parish life after over two hundred years.

As a postscript to the ending of the parish poor law the closing of the workhouse led to yet another spatter of the old charity and rates conflict. The parish quickly let the charity field and the workhouse to the drunken Cashfield at £25 per annum, continuing to pay the vicar £12 as rent for the field, and pocketing the difference. However during the investigation of the Charity Commissioners the Commission pointed out that this could not continue indefinitely and directed that the splitting of the rent should only continue for a limited period, and that thereafter the whole rents of the field and the house should be paid to the Charity. No doubt the spirit of Mr Parfect rejoiced over this end to the long dispute, but one wonders why the charity later sold the house and field, thus losing the advantage of Lady Page's well-thought-out investment in land.

## Chapter 17
## THE RETURN OF THE LORDS OF COBHAM HALL

By the middle of the eighteenth century the major part of the village lands were in the hands of three principal families: the Gordons as the new lords of the manor, the Maplesdens with their Ifield and Pipes Place estates, and the Ayersts, related to the Maplesdens, owning Fullers and a considerable area in and around Shorne Ridgeway. Other families, while still gentry, were less prominent. The Baynards held their lands in Thong and Shorne Ifield, Cheneys Farm in the early eighteenth century belonged to a London family known as Perrins, and Randall Manor had been sold by the Duke of Richmond's descendants to Captain Porten. On Shorne Ridgeway a Mr & Mrs Holmes had a scattered estate of small holdings, some derived from Mrs Holmes' grandfather George Startup, the tanner.

A number of smaller holdings of yeoman style were still scattered around the parish, though their histories are now difficult to establish, but something of the story of the mill has survived and justifies some comment. Shorne windmill had stood on Shorne Hill since the fourteenth century, but by the eighteenth century it was part of the estate of Richard Watts of Rochester, the founder of Watts charity, and from his death was vested in the Mayor and Corporation of Rochester as trustees. They let it to a succession of millers, whose names seldom survive in our records, being always referred to as 'the miller' – even the one who was fined for not attending church.

In 1776 both Richard Hayes of Cobham and later Pocock the Gravesend historian record in their diaries that the mill was struck by lightning and burnt out. Mr Hales walked over from Cobham to inspect the damage and remarks that it looked as if a barrel of gunpowder had been exploded in the mill, and that Mr Bilboe, the miller, was extremely lucky not to have been in the mill when it was struck. He also observed that a great many people on foot and on horseback had come to see the damage, and that a box had been set up for a collection for Mr Bilboe and his family. The mill was soon rebuilt and will again be mentioned in a later chapter.

It is not necessary for the purposes of this history to follow the complicated steps by which the estates of the Duke of Richmond passed into the hands of the Irish John Bligh, who became the first Earl of Darnley. Suffice it to say that by the middle of the eighteenth century the Earl of Darnley had his seat at Cobham Hall, with large estates in Cobham and the surrounding areas. In Shorne however his holding was restricted to the manor of Merston and Green, or Green Farm as it was by then, and marshland at the northern end of the parish. He also seems to have become the owner of Shorne Wood, which though mentioned as part of Shorne Manor in 1407 seems to have become quite removed from the Shorne Manor complex after the fall of Lord Cobham in 1603.

The first opportunity of enlarging the Darnley estates came in 1774, after the death of the Revd William Ayerst. His son, Robert Gunsley Ayerst, already owned the estate in and around Shorne Ridgeway which he had bought from the Revd Buttenshaw, who had purchased it from Martha Woodyear. Robert Gunsley Ayerst was, like his father and grandfather, a clergyman, though until be became vicar of Speldhurst in 1789 he seems to have lived the life of a country gentleman. When his father died he found the three to four hundred acres which comprised his own and his father's lands more than he wanted, and in 1778 he began negotiations with the Earl of Darnley for the sale of the Ridgeway parts of the estate which, as he points out in his first letter to his Lordship, were convenient to 'your Lordship's Park Pale'. The land thus acquired by Lord Darnley consisted of a fairly compact block extending from Park Pale westward along the old Roman Road, until it was bounded by the woodlands of Brewers Wood, which formed part of the Cobham Hall estate.

Soon after this purchase Lord Darnley had another opportunity to enlarge his Shorne estates. Captain Porten of Randall Manor died in 1711 and was buried as of right in the Randall Chapel. After his death the manor and its lands passed through several hands until 1793 when its then owner sold the manor, quit rents, and associated lands to the Earl. Even after two or three generations the names of many of the fields seem to have been associated with Captain Porten. Besides such ordinary names as Windmill Hill Field, we find Cable Wood, Deck Field, Half Deck Field, Forecastle Field, Round House Field, and Anchor Wood, clearly named by the Captain. This added a block of lands close to the Darnley-owned Shorne Wood.

Nearby in Thong was Cheneys Farm, and at the upper end of Thong Lane near St Thomas Well another small holding known as Farmers Hoath. John Reed, the licensee of the See Ho, owned Farmers Hoath in the midcentury, and in 1792 when Cheneys Farm came on the market he bought the two hundred or so acres belonging to that farm.

We may pause for a moment to note the rise in status of John Reed. The Revd Parfect notes him as licensee of the See Ho and that 'some drunken folks must share in the charity thro' Reeds civility to them and his own interest as a publican', but when he died in 1803 John Reed's will reveals that he not only owned Farmers Hoath and Cheneys Farm, but also the Bull Inn at St Mary Cray, 80 acres of land in Chalk called Hungers, a new built house and 24 acres of land in Shorne in his own occupation with two messuages adjoining, three messuages near the windmill, cottages on Shorne Ridgeway, the White Horse at Thong near Cheneys Farm, 34 acres of fresh marsh at Shorne, and the lease of the Cobham tithes. In addition to these properties, all specifically bequeathed, he gave cash legacies of several thousand pounds. Finally he describes himself in his will as 'Gentleman'. One wonders how the See Ho could have provided this wealth. Like John Stone who a century before had been the host of the White Horse in Shorne Street, he must have found the trade of publican remarkably profitable. We may perhaps wonder if the rumours of smuggling which still drift round the village (as they do in almost every village on or near the coast of England) have any basis in fact.

When John Reed died his sons lost no time in disposing of his lands and Lord Darnley picked up the two holdings so conveniently near his Cobham estates. In 1804 he purchased Farmers Hoath and Cheneys Farm, leaving one memorial to Mr Reed which survives in Thong, where a barn belonging to Cheneys Farm was still known as Reeds Barn until a year or so ago, when it was converted into a private house.

The next step in this saga of estate expansion by the house of Darnley concerns lands on the Ridgeway which were acquired by the tanner George Startup a century or so before. These had passed to his granddaughter, Sarah Holmes, whose daughter (also Sarah) married a Mr Bevan. The whole estate is well defined in a fine estate map prepared in 1781, but by 1800 the estate had been split up and most of it sold to the Earl of Darnley.[1]

Whilst this was going on Shorne Manor and its estates were passing from one member of the Gordon family to another. Thomas Gordon did not live long to enjoy his new manor, for he died in 1756 leaving his estate to his daughter Elizabeth. She married her cousin William Gordon of Rochester who had managed the estate on behalf of his uncle. He was a wine merchant (one of Mr Parfect's letters to him mentions that Mr Parfect's wine bins were empty). On the marriage in 1761 the usual settlement was entered into whereby the manor and its estates were settled on Elizabeth for life and then passed to her children. There was only one child of the marriage, a daughter also named Elizabeth. William Gordon died in 1780 and the two Elizabeths entered into further settlements when the daughter came of age which, whilst preserving the interests of the mother, enabled the daughter on her marriage in 1783 to Samuel Barrett, a Captain in the 37th Regiment of Foot, to resettle the estate once again.

This last settlement contained the seeds of the final dissolution of the manor estate. It provided in the usual way for a life interest for the daughter with a reversion to any children of the marriage, but there was also a provision that in the event of the death of the daughter without issue, Captain Barrett should have a life interest in the estate, subject of course to the already existing life interest of his mother-in-law. The daughter did die without issue and the Captain only had to wait for his mother-in-law to die to come into possession of the estate.

Elizabeth the mother seems to have been active in village affairs, taking over the Receivership of the Page charity on her husband's death. She died in 1807, bequeathing the estate, subject to her son-in-law's life interest, to trustees for sale. The son-in-law had in the meantime married again and taken up residence at Court Lodge. Not surprisingly litigation followed the death of Mrs Gordon. After some negotiation the Court ordered that the estate be sold, and that Captain Barrett, who was then said to be fifty-seven years of age, should have forty pounds in every hundred of the sale price, and three pounds in every hundred for the timber. Since the estate was said to be worth at least thirty thousand pounds, the Captain seems to have secured a very good bargain from his first shortlived marriage.

Tanyard Hill looking south: a photograph taken some thirty years ago.

On 27th September 1814 the whole estate was auctioned at the Crown Hotel, Rochester, in sixteen lots. One gets the impression that the sale was an event patronised by all, and the bidding was confused. The Earl of Darnley was naturally a keen bidder, and had the whole estate been submitted in one lot there is little doubt that he would have acquired it. But this did not happen and the various lots were knocked down to various bidders of whom the Earl was only one. Indeed so confused was the result that the Court ordered several lots to be re-submitted and after the further auction and much post-sale negotiation Lord Darnley acquired the manor and most of the estate, roughly the whole of its southern part where it adjoined the Earl's existing holdings, but Court Lodge and some of the surrounding lands passed to Captain Barrett — by this time known as Tufnell Barrett.

To return to the Ayerst estates, Robert Gunsley Ayerst, having sold his Ridgeway lands to the Earl of Darnley, settled comfortably into his Fullers estate, and though he was Rector of Speldhurst from 1787 until his death, he kept up his association with the village, and when he died gave a substantial legacy to the parish for the establishment of a Sunday school — a matter we shall deal with later. He had outlived his contemporaries when he died in 1816 at the age of 94, a grandson of Thomas Ayerst, vicar of Shorne in the reign of Charles II.

Fullers passed to his grandson, who adopted the name of Robert Gunsley Ayerst (to confuse the geneaologists), and then went to live at Bath. In 1828 he sold the bulk of the Fullers estate to Lord Darnley, leaving the remainder — the old house Fullers and small adjoining fields — to be the subject of litigation which was not settled until the end of the century.

The same view of Tanyard Hill today. It may be observed that in this and the preceding five plates the scene can be identified by the pollarded willow trees which appear in each picture. These are the survivors of a 'willow plat' mentioned in documents of the 18th century.

Thus by the late 1820s the only substantial blocks of land in the parish not in Darnley hands were the Maplesden estates of Ifield Court and Pipes Place, and the small estate around Court Lodge held by the Tufnell Barretts. After the death of the last Jarvis Maplesden his estates passed to his sisters, and finally to a granddaughter of Jarvis Maplesden V. She married Jarvis Noakes, and had ten or eleven children. This complicated devolution could not go on, and in 1870 the inheritance was sold. The Earl of Darnley purchased Ifield Court, thus rounding off the ownership of the farms and woodlands of Shorne from Park Pale to Clay Lane Woods on the south, as far north as the Gravesend-Rochester Road, with Green Farm and marshlands by the river. Only small patches, the largest of which was Court Lodge, were left in other hands.

The result of this expansion of the Darnley estates was to remove from village life all the substantial landowners who had lived there and participated in village affairs for a couple of centuries. The Woodyears, the Gordons, the Ayersts, and above all the Maplesdens, had in their several ways lived in the village, joined in its affairs, attended its vestries and the church, given legacies to village charities, and finally rested within the walls of the church. Throughout the nineteenth century this was changed. The landed influence in the village became that of the Lords of Cobham Hall, who were remote from village affairs. A steward, who seems always to have lived at Thong or Shorne Ifield, and the larger tenant farmers of the Darnley farms, took the place of the local small squires.

1. Another trap for the placename students. The estate included a small farm now called 'Bushey Leas' – it being assumed the 'leas' referred to its being a 'lea' of scrub. In the map and the deeds it is called 'Bushy Leaves'.

The Old Vicarage. Given to the parish by Thomas Page in 1495, it was for some four centuries the home of the vicars. Now in private ownership after much alternation during the centuries it still contains much of its original structure.

Court Lodge. Beneath the regency style exterior which was erected by the Tufnell Barrett family in the early 19th century was the old red brick Court Lodge occupied in the 17th century by the Woodyear family, then lords of the manor of Shorne.

## Chapter 18
## THE LAST DAYS OF THE MANOR

As an epilogue to the changing ownership of the lands of the parish there is a small collection of manorial documents from the early nineteenth century at the Kent County Archive office which, though by then quite archaic in form, mark the ending of what had once been so important a part of village life.

By this time the Manor of Shorne and the Hundred of Shamwell had become merged, and the View of Frankpledge and Court Baron dealt with matters affecting the hundred as well as the manor. As a result the Court held at the Beef Steak House, presided over by the Steward of the Lord, was attended by a few villagers from the neighbouring parishes of Higham, Chalk, Cobham, Strood and Cooling, if for no other reason than that the jury of the court elected the High Constables of the hundred and such officers for these villages as were usually appointed by the old hundred.

So far as Shorne Manor was concerned, the jury, which usually numbered a dozen or so local yeomen, elected three borsholders for the north, west and south boroughs of the manor, an aletaster, a hayward, and a street driver. Even then the aletaster must have been an anachronism, since two of the Shorne inns were already leased by the Becket brothers, brewers of Gravesend, and used as tied houses. The courts do not seem to have been held regularly and one gets the impression that the appointment of officers was rather the formality of finding names to fill an office, than the selection of officers from a press of candidates.

The rolls contained long lists of quit rents, and records of changes of ownership of the lands charged, but the rents, based on the settlement of 1407, were small and hardly worth collecting in some cases. The principal concern of the manor court seems to have been the management of the Shorne Mead common marsh grazing. This again was an anomally. The grazing was not common to the whole of the manor tenantry. Only the owners of certain lands in the parish had the right to graze their animals there. The vicar of Shorne had nearly three acres as part of his glebe, as had the Maplesdens as part of their estates. All are said to be owners of specific areas of marsh land, though as the areas were not enclosed in any way the acreages seem to have been a guide to the number of animals the owner of the land could put on the common marsh.

The court spent much time settling the rules and orders for the better regulation of the Mead. In 1819 for instance the jury declared that the byelaws relating to the Mead were difficult to ascertain, and therefore revoked all former rules and adopted a new set which were set out at length in the court roll.

The rules provide for the appointment of an 'Expenditor', who had the management of the Mead, the times when grazing and haymaking were permitted, and how many cattle should be turned out on the Mead. His expenses of repairing gates, fences and roads were assessed against each commoner at a small sum, which was increased by a charge of fourpence for a bullock and penny for a sheep at the gate as the animal was driven in. The 'Expenditor' also got a further fee of one shilling for every bullock he should draw or take out of any ditch. The dates of entry and so on were then announced in church on the Sunday following the manor court.

In the first two decades of the nineteenth century the management and use of the Mead, and indeed the remainder of the marshland grazing which for many centuries had been so important a part of village agriculture, was interrupted by the construction of the Thames and Medway Canal. The line of the canal crossed the marshes from east to west and had the effect of severing the grazing areas into two parts, leaving access between them at only two points; the Stonewick Bridge, which crossed the canal at roughly the point where the older road to Lower Higham led to Higham Causeway, and the other the unnamed bridge near Queens Farm which was the point where the ancient manor way to Shorne Mead came to the marsh. Thus was ended the older broad driving of animals from the farms further inland across old droveways convenient to each farm.

The manor court from time to time also dealt with encroachments upon the manor estates. It must be remembered that the manor had wide areas of wastelands, usually bordering the roads. For instance there was a long strip of waste belonging to the manor on the north side of the old road between Shorne Ridgeway and a point somewhere near St Thomas's Well. As early as 1668 William Woodyear had granted to John Birt, the then owner of Farmers Hoath near Thong Lane, the right to enclose part of this waste, while the residue remained waste until the beginning of the nineteenth century. There was much other land at the sides of other village roads which was 'waste' in the sense that it was not cultivated or used for any special purpose except the casual browsing of villagers' animals.

By the 1820s however this sort of thing was no longer accepted by the farmers of the lands adjoining the 'wastes'. When William Phillips made an encroachment of the waste by enclosing and laying into a field then belonging to Sarah Bevan on Shorne Ridgeway between the See Ho and Bushey Leas, he was presented at the manor court and enjoined to give up what he had taken. He seems to have taken no notice, for there is now no road verge on that side of the road, though oddly enough opposite this particular spot there is still a strip of roadside verge by the site of Little Moor Farm and the old tanyard. The owner of Little Moor had earlier built a substantial brick wall to enclose his yard, leaving the waste by the roadside, and it was afterwards not worth anyone's while to pull down the wall to take the waste into the field. The map of the Holmes estate shows the 'waste' taken by Mrs Bevan's tenant as at least as wide as the still unenclosed land opposite.

The manor also had two areas of common land quite distinct from the marsh grazing or the 'waste'. At the beginning of the nineteenth century these consisted of one area some six or seven acres in extent on Shorne Hill, and the other a larger less well defined area of perhaps ten or twelve acres on the Ridgeway, centred around the junction of Woodlands Lane (then called Back Lane) and Shorne Ridgeway, consisting of a traingular area, now a worked out gravel pit, and lands on the southern side of the Ridgeway near Puckle Hill. Probably in medieval times the two areas were one common. The Shorne Hill common still has an extension, road-like in width, called Green Lane, which points across the gravelly fields of Scammels[1] towards the Ridgeway common, the two areas being still connected by footpaths.

The commons were just as likely to be nibbled at by adjoining landowners as the wastes, and an action in the courts which arose shortly after Lord Darnley acquired the manor not only illustrates this but also gives some idea of the place which commons and common rights had in the lives of the ordinary villagers.

The Green Lane extension of the Shorne Hill common was bounded on the south east side by land belonging to Mr Comport. In 1816 he grubbed up the fence, levelled the bank and ditch which separated his land from the common, and enclosed about an acre of Green Lane. He was presented before the manor court, and the fence was pulled down. Mr Comport at once re-erected the fence and Lord Darnley, 'considering this an act of impudent aggression' as the brief to Counsel says, directed his bailiff John Copelin to pull down the fence once again and throw it on Mr Comport's land. This done Mr Comport issued a writ for trespass against Mr Copelin which was set down to be heard at the Kent Assizes.

The brief to Counsel on behalf of Mr Copelin (backed of course by Lord Darnley) then gives a number of statements by local witnesses which throw interesting light on the usage of the common by the parish, and the Lord of the Manor.

The common, including Green Lane, was covered by scrub, except where gravel digging pockmarked the surface. One gravel pit was actually at the end of the piece of land enclosed by Mr Comport. William French, who had been Mrs Gordon's steward and agent until she died in 1807, stated that long before he took office in 1782 there was a gravel pit on the common, and that as Mrs Gordon's agent he had sold gravel to Mr Brandon the surveyor of the turnpike road from Strood to Dartford, and received anything between six pounds and fourteen pounds a year from this source. He also sold gravel to anyone who wanted it at a shilling a waggon or sixpence a cart load. Parishioners however were allowed to take the gravel for themselves without charge.

Of greater importance to the poorer element of the village was the scrub. Several witnesses give their own version of this right, but all agree that the scrub growth on the common was freely taken, as of right, by any villager for fuel. Indeed it seems to have been the principal source of fuel for the poor. Richard Marshall, a village labourer aged 65 who had been employed by Mr Barrett to supervise on his behalf the taking of gravel from the hill when Mr Barrett was still life tenant of the manor, said that when he was a boy his mother would send him to the common to cut scrub to heat her oven. He had cut scrub from each side of Green Lane.

Mr French in his evidence said that Green Lane was mostly covered with scrub and that he had had to cut it back to enable his waggons with timber from Randall Wood to pass with the waggoners walking by the horses, and remarked that he did not take the cut scrub but left it by the sides of the lane, and it was later taken by the poor.

This was the recollection of the older inhabitants, but other evidence indicates that the custom was not always accepted by the adjoining farmers. Richard Cashfield, whom we have already met, gave evidence that he used to take scrub when a boy, but on one occasion he was stopped by Richard Sawyer, the predecessor of Mr Comport. 'He told me if he ever caught me cutting wood again he would beat me' was Cashfield's comment. Another witness named Cripps also told how when cutting scrub on the opposite side of Green Lane he had been stopped by Noakes, the tenant on that side, and that Noakes took his wood bill away from him.

From all this it is clear that amongst the changes of the early nineteenth century was the decay of the older casual life of the rural seventeenth and eighteenth centuries, with the simple economics of the life of the poorer people, the freely available fuels (poor as it might be), and their casual grazing of animals on the waste, being steadily suppressed.

Yet these rights were tenaciously held. I have been told by one villager that his father had always told him that he had always taken wood, as of right, from Shorne Common Rough on the Ridgeway. Likewise, until the full flood of the motor vehicle on the roads, the tethering of ponies and goats on the small patches of remaining waste went on until the present century.

The real end of the manor of Shorne as an entity with any meaning came with the enclosure of Shorne Mead in 1845, when the few commoners with rights over the meadows were awarded portions. Shortly afterwards the severance of the marsh by the canal was completed by the construction of the South Eastern and Chatham Railway along the line of the canal. and a little later the whole mead was acquired by the War Office as part of the Milton Ranges. Finally in the 1880s by mutual arrangement Lord Darnley and his manorial tenants cleared off the quit rents by redemption. By that time all reason for manor courts had ceased, and the manor had become an antiquarian memory.

1. Scammels is the name attached to an area of fields on the ridge connecting Shorne Hill to the high woodlands at the south of the parish. The ancient hundred name of Shamwell was once Escammels, and it seems possible this was once the site of the ancient hundred courts.

## Chapter 19
## THE CHURCH AND SCHOOL

After the passing of so dominant a character as the Revd Caleb Parfect, his successors seem to have been shadowy absentees. The Ven. John Law, Archdeacon of Rochester and a notable pluralist, held the living for seven years after Mr Parfect's death. He was followed by the Revd Peter Pinner who was vicar from 1777 to 1782, holding also the living at Eltham, and a prebend at Rochester. Then came the Revd Henry Jones, vicar from 1783 to 1799, and Revd Robert Foote, vicar from 1799 to 1804. The Revd Foote also held a prebend at Rochester and was the incumbent of Boughton Malherbe, where he was buried. Of them only the Revd Jones seems to have given regular attention to local church affairs, the duties of the vicars being normally carried out by a curate with the help of the parish clerk.

There is a churchwarden's account book from 1781 to 1795, which is sadly much less informative than the account of the previous century, and marks the decreasing lay importance of the churchwarden's office. Only his duties as a pest control officer seem to have survived, and the pests have changed significantly. Foxes and badgers have practically disappeared, but hedgehogs, pole-cats, and sparrows take their place. The harmless hedgehog had fourpence on his head, the pole-cat was equally low priced, whilst the sparrow was paid for at three pence a dozen. Large numbers of sparrows were regularly accounted for. An average year would account for some three or four hundred, but in 1789 for some undisclosed reason the total toll was over a thousand.

The accounts do not help much with the church itself. From other sources we can trace something of what was done in and around the building. The low steeple on the tower seems to have been removed and the present lead roof of the tower installed in about 1768 from the date on the leads. The ancient wooden shingles were also replaced during this period by clay tiles, and when the accounts begin in 1781 there are references to winding the clock, which suggests that this prominent part of village life was installed between the passing of the Revd Parfect — we cannot imagine him letting such an occasion go by without at least a latin tag — and the beginning of the accounts. In 1805 the bells which had hung in the tower from the end of the fifteenth century were taken down and recast.

The normal church duties of the churchwardens go on as before. The visitations, (though a churchwarden's dinner now usually cost about thirty shillings), bread and wine purchased, bell ringers paid a 'noble' for their efforts on Gunpowder Treason day and King's birthday, bell ropes purchased, all appear as they had done a hundred years earlier, but the 'bills' for 'work done' conceal any repairs to the church. We know that the church was frequently whitewashed inside, from the remark of Dr Harris in his antiquarian notes that the interior of

An old picture of the Randall Chapel when it was used as a schoolroom. The fireplace, various forms and other school fittings are interesting.

School house which replaced the school room in the church. Now the site of two houses.

the building had been so bestowed with whitewash, that the font and the effigy of Sir Henry de Cobham resembled lumps of chalk.

The arrival of William Tolbutt Staines as vicar in 1805 begins another period in which the vicar leaves his mark on parish affairs. Without in any way approaching Mr Parfect's copious notes, he kept records in the registers of such matters as the appointment of the parish clerk, and the fact that two more chestnut trees had been planted on each side of the churchyard gate — they are both gone now.

Some of Mr Staines' entries concern the choir and music in the church services. It will be remembered Mr Parfect had agreed to the employment of a teacher for the singers, and one of the items in the ten years of churchwardens' accounts at the end of the eighteenth century is the regular payment to Master Hills for 'learning the singers'.

It seems that when Mr Staines came to the parish he found there was some grumbling discontent in the congregation about the whole business. The music in the church was then led by a small group of musicians with two clarionets, two bassoons, and a bass viol. Apparently village talent did not produce a player of the bass viol and the vicar had endeavoured to get one from outside. He also seems to have increased the number of sung psalms in the services.

Things came to a head on the first Sunday of July 1815, when several of the congregation left the church in the middle of the service. Mr Staines drew up a set of rules concerning the music in the church which he submitted to the Bishop for his approval. The Bishop replied quickly. He condemned 'Those who behaved in so indecent and offensive a manner' as to leave the service, and then picked his way through the proposed rules with comments which enable us to visualise something of the church services at the time.

The prime trouble seems to have been the admission of strangers to the 'singers and performers'. The Bishop approved a rule that the singers and performers should all be villagers, with a provision that non-parishioners be occasionally allowed for such as a master of singers or a performer on the bass viol. He also saw no objection to the five instruments. Mr Staines' rules detailed what singing was to be permitted. He provided for a Jubilate immediately after the second lesson. He also wanted an anthem or psalm between the reading of the psalms and the first lesson, but the Bishop pointed out that this was not in the rubric, and though he personally had no objection, thought it should be avoided. In the evening the bishop approved the Magnificat being sung after the first lesson, and a psalm after the third collect. He also approved an anthem or psalm being sung after the prayers of the day if there should be a sermon in the afternoon. Finally he agreed a further rule that a psalm should be sung before the communion service if that service was accompanied by a sermon.

It seems that these arrangements about the musicians were not fully accepted by the congregation, because two years later Mrs Keating, a relative of the Ayersts, presented the church with a barrel organ, which replaced the orchestra in the gallery at the west end of the church.

Mr Staines' incumbency, however, is chiefly to be remembered for its foundation of the Shorne church school — with its hope for the future — in the same decade as the building of the workhouse and the flogging of the idle.

What schooling the villagers had in the eighteenth century is not known. The standard of literacy of the parish officers was fairly constant, most signing their names to the accounts, and though some only made their mark, again many wrote out the whole accounts themselves, and one must assume that there was generally some rural pundit who ran a Dame's school for those wishing to learn to read and write, but unable to aspire to the King's School or the Mathematical School at Rochester.

In February 1816 the Revd Robert Gunsley Ayerst died, and by his will bequeathed £1,000 3% Consolidated Stock to the parish, the dividends to be used for the maintenance of a Sunday School for the education of the poor children of Shorne. Education was at this time becoming an interest of the Church of England. The National Society had been formed in 1811, so the time was ripe. When the news of the legacy — a handsome one by any standards — became known, a meeting of the parishioners was called under the guidance of the Revd Staines, and it was resolved that:—

'The inhabitants of and others connected by property with the Parish of Shorne . . . acknowledging the great benefits to be derived in the community from an early education of its members rightly directed, have entered into a subscription for the purpose of establishing a school in order to instruct the poor children of that place in the rudiments of knowledge agreeable to their condition and in the principles of the Church of England according to the plan recommended by the Revd Dr Bell.'

Some twenty-seven resolutions follow this unctuous beginning, of which we need only mention that it was agreed the school be opened on the 25th March 1816, and that Mr John Tomlin be appointed schoolmaster with a salary of £60 per annum.

A subscription list was opened and annual subscriptions totalling over forty-two pounds (headed by ten guineas from the Earl of Darnley) were promised. Later donations and subscriptions produced another fifteen pounds or so, whilst a collection at the church door in April produced another £4.9.6d. In order to raise further funds it was agreed to have a weekly payment (later fixed at two-pence) from the children of the parish who attended, and that children from outside the parish should be admitted 'upon terms to be regulated by the committee'. Even with these funds it was thought they would not be adequate to enable a mistress to be appointed to assist John Tomlin, but it was hoped further efforts would provide the necessary money. Finally, until a permanent school-room could be provided, it was proposed by Mr Tomlin that a room in his house should be used, the rent to be paid for this room being left unsettled.

The Revd Ayerst's idea of a Sunday school was absorbed in this wider arrangement and his legacy income applied towards the general schooling proposed in the resolution. The only concession to his idea was a resolution (amongst a long list of resolutions fixing the hours of attendance at school and the length of school holidays) which provided that the Shorne children attending the day school should attend the morning and afternoon services at the parish church every Sunday, and such other services as were held. The master was to attend every Sunday both before and after divine service, and carefully instruct the children in the church catechism and other religious knowledge according to the practice of Sunday schools of the Church of England.

On the 25th March twenty-nine boys and thirty girls were enrolled under the 'Poor' category, whilst seven other children of more respectable parents were admitted at five shillings a quarter. The Treasurer was authorised to provide slates, books and stationery. A week later the school was formally inspected by the whole committee — for a time the committee seems to have treated the establishment with something of the enthusiasm of a child with a new toy — two or three children were added to the roll, and a long list of rules was drawn up to be exhibited in some conspicuous part of the school.

It is at this point we realise from several of the rules that from the beginning in spite of the original proposal to use a room in Mr Tomlin's house, the school was held in the church. After the loquaciousness of the minutes it is surprising there is no record of the old Randall chapel being furnished and fitted up as a school-room. There is a possible explanation of this in an otherwise unsupported story that the old chapel had in fact been used as a schoolroom from 1771, and may already have had the desks and benches which furnished the new school. Rules providing that the children were to keep to the gravel walk to the church and that the schoolmaster was to see the children did not remain in the church after school hours are the first indication that the chapel was in use. Later that year there are references to a partition being raised to separate the school room from the 'prospect of the inside of the church', and this was supported by a grant of £20 from the National Society.

The numbers attending the school increased steadily and neighbouring parishes began to send their children to the school, indicating the growing desire for education, and the inadequacy of the provision for it in neighbouring villages. These 'foreigners' were charged three pence per week, or ten shillings and sixpence a quarter.

With the increase in pupils the committee's hope to appoint a school mistress was fulfilled in November 1816, when Mrs Botting was nominated to attend the school until a permanent mistress be chosen. She was replaced by a curious arrangement in December when the committee appointed Sarah Tomlin (daughter of the master) to be a teacher under the mistress and that Mrs Tomlin be elected as the mistress — a notable example of 'keeping it in the family'. The funds available, however, only allowed Mrs Tomlin to be paid fifteen pounds per annum, and it seems Miss Tomlin simply 'helped mother' for nothing.

After the Revd Staines left the parish the minutes of the school committee slowly fade away, there being no minute after 1840. By that time the school

The mill converted into an observation platform.

The later mill building before it was burnt down in 1952.

seems to have become a well-attended organisation with some one hundred and fifty children from Shorne and the surrounding villages.

We are fortunate in having a sketch of the school-room made in the mid-nineteenth century showing a fireplace in the southern wall (with the master's desk significantly near the fire), a raised bench and desks along the eastern wall under the window where no doubt the senior children sat, with a scatter of forms in the rest of the room. An old lady of the village (she has been dead many years now), probably the last survivor of those who received their education there, told me that all she could remember of the school was 'Those old grave stones were mortal cold: they used to give us the ague'. The children had their revenge. The constant treading of their hobnailed boots has worn away nearly all the inscriptions on the few slabs that now remain in the chapel.

## Chapter 20
## VICTORIAN SHORNE

A good introduction to the Victorian period in Shorne village is Bagshaws History Gazetteer and Directory for Kent, published in 1847, which not only gives a list of the principal inhabitants, but also a number of topographical details.

Of the landowners the principal ones were the Trustees of the Earl of Darnley and Tufnell Carbonel Barrett. Other landowners are mentioned but they did not live in the village and form no part of this story.

In a previous chapter we have recorded the manoeuvres which left Samuel Tufnell Barrett as the owner of the old Court Lodge and the lands around, but the Gazetteer enlightens us on what had followed. Samuel Tufnell Barrett's heir Tufnell Carbonel Barrett had not only rebuilt the house but had 'laid out and beautified the ground in the vicinity of the house with great taste; the ground only a few years ago an impossible bog is now covered with most luxuriant fertility'. He had also added many 'Neat Swiss and Elizabethan cottages, which give to the part of the village near his residence an air of rural and picturesque beauty'. This involved the clearance of the farm buildings, oasts and tanyard which had formed part of the old Court Lodge background.

The Court Lodge which was pulled down some fifteen years ago was the house built by the Barretts on and around the older smaller farm house previously occupied by the Lords of the Manor, which from the portions which had been incorporated into the newer building seems to have been a small red brick Georgian house. The Barrett house was a building of considerable size, but little real charm. The stuccoed mansion had a sort of Regency exterior, but within it had oak panelling, and an oak staircase, supplemented by a mass of ornamental plaster painted to resemble wood panelling; the whole having a somewhat exotic air.

After the principal landowners the Gazetteer has a list of inhabitants, restricted mainly to the tradespeople. Here we find two butchers, three bakers (two of them also grocers), two wood dealers, two boot and shoe makers, two cow-keepers and some seven farmers, as well as the miller, a blacksmith, a wheelwright, and the tanner. It is also a little surprising to find a tailor and a dressmaker.

Recently when clearing out the upper floor of a house in the Street now known as Homemead Cottage, a mass of clippings from materials of all descriptions, buttons, cotton reels and other debris of a tailor was found under the floor and some years ago I was told by an old villager that a Mr Walker, the village tailor, lived there. He is the tailor named in the Gazetteer.

Though there are seven tenant farmers noted in the Directory, the real power in the farming world of the village was that of the Solomon family. The

Shorne Mill in working order about 1880.

origin of the family is not clear. At the beginning of the century Joseph and Elizabeth Solomon came to the village from elsewhere, and their several children's births are recorded. By 1847 Joseph Solomon farmed Queens Farm, his brother Henry farmed at Thong and a third brother Thomas farmed Green farm. Though only tenant farmers this brotherhood ruled the village farm labour for half a century. Any man sacked by one could hardly hope to find employment in a village where the remaining farmers were relatively small yeomen employing little labour. The eldest was known in the village as 'King Solomon' and the family seems to have survived the vicissitudes of the agricultural world of the nineteenth century, to disappear at the turn of the century as suddenly as it had come, leaving only a row of gravestones by the churchyard path to mark its passing.

As a counter to this aspect of rural life we must remember that the Earls of Darnley throughout the nineteenth century provided considerable employment in the district. The boys and young men might look for work in the gardens and park as gardeners and roadmen. A corps of gamekeepers was recruited from all over the district, and during the season much casual employment as beaters and hangers-on at the shoots could be expected to help over the winter. Inside the Hall many old villagers remembered the life 'below stairs' with nostalgic affection. A village girl might well hope to rise from kitchen hand, to chamber maid and the like. Here was a secure, warm, and well-fed life. The hours might cause a modern trade unionist to feel faint, but the period from dawn rising to the late retirement was at a less hectic pace than that of today, and judging from the memories of some villagers, below stairs community activities, like concerts and dances, were frequent and enjoyable. The estate also built three blocks of cottages in the village in the Darnley-favoured mock tudor design which in their day were well ahead of the ordinary cottage in the village for convenience and finish.

These new cottages in no way met the growing population of the village at this time. To meet the demand large old houses were divided into tenements, and apart from the new Darnley cottages, the Tufnell Barretts built not only 'neat Swiss and Elizabethan cottages', but also an undistinguished row of cottages on the Ridgeway called Victoria cottages. The Tufnell Barrett houses have now all been pulled down, but the Darnley cottages are in some demand as country cottages for town dwellers and remain restored and improved.

A Methodist Chapel on Shorne Ridgeway built in 1838 reminds us of an aspect of village life which has so far received little notice — the development of nonconformity in the village. We remember the men who became prominent in the civil war who we suspect were Puritans. Rejoice Head, one of them, christened his son 'Rejoice' but later the family seems to have become a conforming part of the parish community. On the other hand the Pace family present a more connected trace of anabaptist tendencies. Robert Pace is named in the registers as the father of a number of children born between 1656 and 1671, most of whom are entered without christian name, except for one named 'Gartered'. Later a

Zion Chapel, the Methodist chapel built in 1838. The scene in 1950 showing Victoria Cottages (now demolished).

member of the family is called 'Fear God' Pace, though she may well be one of the unnamed children in the registers.

In 1682 Thomas Glover's child 'yt died unbaptised' was 'put into ye ground by ye clerk' and a little later in 1689 and 1690 children of William Lessiter were buried in the common burial place 'unbaptised'. At the turn of the century Richard Pollington, a tailor by trade, comes into the registers. In 1699 the vicar records in the register of baptisms 'Ricardus Pollington Adultus (ex Anabaptistii)' and in 1701 the vicar records the baptism of a child of Richard Pollington 'taylor and anabaptist'. There is a faint connection between the Paces, Lessiters and Pollingtons, in that, one or other of them occasionally appears as the person making the affidavit of 'buried in wool' for a member of the other families.

After this there are no clear indications of any further declared dissenters in the parish except that in the churchwardens' accounts in 1787 is recorded the payment of twelve shillings and six pence 'expenses of getting a Quaker's rate'. The Quaker is not named, but it seems likely that this was William Cleverly the Northfleet shipbuilder who had just purchased Little Moors and was a known Quaker.

Perhaps the trouble in the church over the Revd Staines' changes in music in the church may have had some potential dissenting background, but the Chapel on the Ridgeway is the first clear indication of the growth of methodism in the village. There is an interesting tradition about the building of the chapel. Old villagers said that this chapel was built by John Clark, a villager who is mentioned in the Gazetteer as a woodman. The story whispered around the village was that though but a poor wood cutter, John Clark suddenly produced enough money not only to build the chapel but also a large house on the Ridgeway opposite, now called **Ridgeway House**, the money being derived from a hidden treasure of gold which he had found while working in the woods.

Some of his descendants still live in the village, but wryly comment that if he ever found a treasure he did not leave any of it for his descendants. I suspect that in fact he was one of those characters often associated with nonconformity, who by careful attention to business and hard work, accumulate money in less romantic ways than finding buried treasure. During his life he and his family worshipped in the chapel under his patriarchal rule.

There was also some further dissent in the village in the nineteenth century about which we would like to know more. In 1887 it appears that a group of 'dissenters' began to hold services on waste land on the Ridgeway. The vicar, greatly annoyed, wrote to Lord Darnley as Lord of the Manor to know if he had given permission for this 'indecent' use of manor waste. His Lordship's trustees at once replied that they certainly did not approve, and gave the vicar full authority to see that such things did not happen again. The trustee's letter has survived, and it would be interesting to know more about these bold dissenters. Later the Plymouth Brethren had a chapel in a cottage on the Ridgeway, but no connection can be proved.

The obstruction of the Thames and Medway Canal has already been mentioned. It was never a success as a shipping short cut between Thames and Medway, and in 1841 the Canal Company, in an attempt to profit from the immense popularity of Gravesend as a pleasure resort at that time, constructed a single track railway from the Canal Basin at Gravesend to the Canal Basin at Strood. This of course further interfered with the use of the marshland grazing, and may well have been a factor in the enclosing of the Common marsh in 1845. The South Eastern and Chatham Railway, which was then laying a line to Gravesend, acquired the canal and immediately constructed a double track line along the canal bank, filling in the canal in the Higham Tunnel to take the double track. This further severed the village from the marshes. Level crossings and faster trains hindered the movement of animals to and from the marsh grazing far more than barges and canal traffic.

The railway had an even greater indirect influence on village life. The life and traffic on the Dover Road died away. The stage coaches, the travelling coaches of the great, the traveller on horse or on foot to East Kent and the continent disappeared. Only local traffic used the road: the long distance traveller used the railway. The wayfarers, already severely restricted by the new poor law and the Unions, were reduced to the passing 'tramp' on his way from one Union Workhouse to another.

During the thirties and forties of the century the village was able to share in the popularity of Gravesend as a holiday centre. The guide books of the town all include pleasant excursions to the surrounding villages, and Shorne is mentioned in all of them. Miss Brabazon's 'A month in Gravesend' published as late as 1863 described the village in quite lyrical terms: 'With its romantic looking old grey house of prayer, girt around with luxuriant foliage and deep masses of orchard bloom' and we can imagine the energetic ramblers of those days being charmed with the 'neat' Swiss and Elizabethan cottages of Tufnell Barrett's construction.

## Chapter 21
## THE LATER VICTORIAN CHURCH

For over fifty years of the nineteenth century, Shorne had another notable vicar in the person of The Revd Jacob Joseph Marsham, son of the Hon. and Revd Jacob Marsham D.D., Canon of Windsor and of Rochester. He was educated at Eton and Christ Church, Oxford, and his family was well connected beyond anything known of our earlier vicars. A bachelor, a 'Squareson' of the old school, (riding boots with spurs could be seen beneath his cassock on Sundays) in his early days he was said to be one of the boldest cross-country riders in the county.

In his funeral oration the Revd Canon Coates, who succeeded him in the living, said his most distinguishing feature was his charitableness and devotion to his church, never allowing anything to keep him from divine worship. Later in life he lost his sight, but according to Canon Coates he remained cheerful and resigned in his affliction.

Villagers who had no aristocratic connections, and did not ride to hounds, remembered a different vicar. Perhaps the best illustration of this is the recollection of one old villager who remembered the vicar old and blind being led round on his horse by his groom, barking out 'Who's that, Potts?' to his groom if passing footsteps did not halt for the woman to curtsey, or the man to touch his hat as he rode by.

Yet whichever view one had of him, there is no doubt that he devoted the whole of his long life to the village. Unlike so many of his predecessors he was not a pluralist, and after living in various rented houses in the village, he finally built his house 'Overblow' where he resided until his death.

Between 1867 and 1887 he was assisted in the work of the parish by the Revd Tuffnell Samuel Barrett, son of the squire of Court Lodge, who had succeeded to Court Lodge on his father's death in 1858, and thus occupied a curious place in parish affairs both as landowner and later as a Justice of the Peace. The bishop's letter approving the Revd Barrett's association with the church (he was, with his position, hardly an ordinary curate) remarks that this was the first letter he had addressed to 'Overblow' which he called, somewhat archly, 'The Temple of the winds', and illustrates the somewhat cosy ecclesiastical connections of those days. Actually the name 'Overblow' is taken from the Revd Marsham's birthplace, Kirkby Overblow in Yorkshire.

The conjunction of these two reverend gentlemen has a memorial in the restoration of the church. In the middle of the century the church must have presented a drab appearance. The north and south chancels were partitioned off to form schoolrooms, whilst the west end of the nave and the tower archway was blocked by a gallery and partitioning, which effectively cut off all light from the tower window. The windows of the church are specially mentioned in the architect's report which preceded the restoration. There were only two windows in the south wall of the south aisle, the eastern one being described as a 'horrid' wooden affair. A similar description was applied to the window in the north chancel, whilst the lancet window in the west wall of the north aisle was blocked with brickwork.

The interior stonework had been scraped, repaired and pointed before the architect made his report 'in a clumsy way' as he describes it — the harsh dark pointing in the south arcade being unhappily still with us. Outside the condition was deplorable. The stonework of the south aisle was badly weathered, and most of the buttresses around the church were a patchwork of brick with cappings of tin or zinc. The Randall Chapel had an east window which the architect describes as 'hideous'. It had apparently been rebuilt in brick in 1771 — according to a date chipped into the brickwork. The south side of the chapel was propped up by three enormous buttresses.

Inside the church was a collection of box pews, some of which continued into the chancel, incorporating the remains of the ancient screen, only waist high, into the pew woodwork. The pulpit and clerk's desk on the right-hand side of the chancel arch dominated the whole. Probably the most elegant items of furniture were the two Chippendale gothic-style chairs given by Mr Gordon in Mr Parfect's time, which we still have.

No matter how drab the interior nothing could be done until the children had their separate school. So in the early 1870s a proper school house was built on land on the Common. Until it was demolished it bore the date 1872 on its fascia, though the architect writing his church report in 1873 seems unaware that the school had replaced the classrooms in the church.

As soon as the children left the church its restoration began. Under the chairmanship of the Revd Barrett a committee organised an extensive refurbishment, and in most respects the church which we have today is the result of their efforts.

The gallery with its matchboarded background was removed and a piece of wall supporting it in the western half of the north arcade was pulled down and a new half arch constructed to match the medieval fragment which remained. The contrast between the new Bath stone of the western half of the arch with the 'clunch' of the eastern half is still very obvious. The 'horrid' wooden windows were replaced with good solid Victorian gothic stone windows matching as nearly as possible the older ones. A third window was cut into the centre of the south wall of the south aisle.

The old Randall Chapel, repaired at such cost in 1675 and again in 1771, was beyond further repair and was pulled down. The new chapel was rebuilt on a narrower plan with the aid of a large donation by Lord Darnley. He was Lord of Randall, and fulfilled his obligations as such. All the pews and the old pulpit were ripped out and new pews were installed by the generosity of the Earl of Darnley. The chancel was reroofed by the Dean and Chapter of Rochester, the Rectors of the parish. Most of the work, however, was done at the expense of the parishioners and is said to have cost over £3,000. Some deplore Victorian restorations but without it we would today have even more problems than those which trouble parishioners. The exterior of the church now bears a very different appearance from its pre-restoration condition. The plentiful brick patching of the exterior has gone, replaced by flint and ragstone, and probably the exterior of the church now has more resemblance to its pre-reformation appearance than it has had for centuries.

During the restoration minor changes took place. Henry de Cobham's effigy which had stood in the north aisle, probably for a century or more, was moved back to the reconstructed Randall Chapel, on a Victorian plinth with an inscription which is said to be a copy of the ancient inscription on the original. The floor of the church, which before the restoration was composed of brick and grave slabs, was replaced by red and black tiles. Most of the gravestones disappeared, probably some being buried beneath the floor. Another curious incident concerned the abortive heating arrangements. The original idea was to instal a large hot air system, with a furnace under the floor of the Randall Chapel, the heat being conducted round the church in brick flues under the floors of the aisle, with perforated metal plates here and there for the heat to pass into the church. A large hole was excavated in the Randall Chapel, and, according to village tradition, coffins containing Sir Henry de Cobham and his descendants were removed to a burial place under the green walk round the south side of the church. The ducts under the floor were laid, and are still there, but at this point the whole scheme fell through, the hole in the Randall Chapel was filled in and tiled over, and such heating as the church received was from coke stoves.

Another change in church affairs which took place at this time was the abolition of the ancient church rate in 1871. From that time the church had to depend on collections (which formed but a small part of church income) and donations from church people. Again we may remark the wide benevolence to the community which the return of the Lords of Cobham Hall brought to the district. The donations for rebuilding and church restoration were not the only benefits the village received. Though Lord Darnley was not a worshipper in Shorne, his yearly donation to church expenses was far larger than any of the gifts by the villagers using the church. Nothing like this had happened since Henry Brook, Lord Cobham, had been committed to the Tower by James I.

A quite different aspect of nineteenth century life in the village must be mentioned. It will be remembered that in Mr Parfect's day cricket had been played on the fields above Swillers Lane. At the beginning of the nineteenth century the village had a strong cricket tradition, playing on a field between 'Overblow' and Shorne Ridgeway. Here it was that a match of something more than local interest was played in 1822 when two teams, one from Shorne composed entirely of members of the family of Botting, some of whose descendants still live in the village, played a side from Cobham composed entirely of members of the Baker family living in that parish. Pocock, the Gravesend historian who records the event, also remarks that Shorne won.

This cricket interest continued into the middle and latter part of the century, when a member of the Darnley family took a team to Australia in 1862. In this

*The old look out in Shorne Woods, said to have been erected by Lord Darnley to watch the liner with his son Ivo Bligh and the 'Ashes' returning from Australia.*

team was a Shorne cricketer, one George Bennett, whose gravestone in Shorne churchyard records his prowess which included playing for Kent.

In 1889 the Revd Jacob Marsham resigned from his long incumbency, though continuing to live at 'Overblow'. His place was filled by the Revd Canon Alfred Lloyd Coates, who had been a minor canon of Rochester Cathedral for some years.

With him came another period of change in church matters, as well as civil affairs, which will form part of the next chapter.

The first matter to engage the attention of Canon Coates on his arrival in the village was the ancient vicarage. The Revd Marsham had allowed the old vicarage to become the cottage in which the church verger lived, and in the view of the new vicar it was fit for nothing else. He at once began providing a more suitable residence, both for himself and his successors. He exchanged some glebe land on Tanyard Hill for land to the west of the church adjoining the Common, and to raise funds not only sold the other pieces of glebe attached to the living (at least they disappear from the parish affairs at about this time) but also sold the old vicarage.

He started a Parish Magazine in 1893 and from his notes and letters in the magazine we can follow the story. He complains that it was two years and eight months from commencing his plans before he could even start laying the foundations. Even when the footings were dug a violent storm washed away the unstable gravel of the subsoil of the site, and his architect advised that the whole site be dug down to cellar depth and a foundation of two feet six inches of concrete be laid before the building was begun. A little later he mentions that a water diviner was called in to find a suitable spot for a well, which reminds us how recent is the modern piped water supply to the village. The building was finally finished in April 1895, and the Revd Coates' comments in the parish magazine are strangely reminiscent of Thomas Page's thoughts when some four hundred years before he had made his bequests 'fro vicar to vicar . . . as long as the world shall endure'. Canon Coates happily put an end to the pious donor's hopes, but was nearly as optimistic. He writes that he thinks his new vicarage will serve for several hundred years 'if the world shall last so long . . . for my successors'. Alas, his hopes lasted only half a century.

Whilst this was going on, other events were further changing the predominance of the church. The ancient chapel of St Katherine had from the seventeenth century been used as a malt house, with a cottage built against the eastern wall. In the 1890s the property (which had once formed part of the Maplesden Pipes Place estate) came on the market. A Gravesend worthy, George Matthews Arnold, a devout Roman Catholic who indulged his personal faith by searching out and restoring any ancient and disused chapel or church he could find in North Kent, bought the chapel, carried out a full restoration, and re-dedicated it to Roman Catholic use. He was already the owner of Pipes Place where members of his family lived, and he pulled down the old cottage against the wall of the chapel and built the house in flint and stone, known as St Katherine's house, in the grounds of the chapel.

During the nineteenth century the Methodist connection in the village grew, a Primitive Methodist circle being formed as a breakaway group from the Clark-dominated chapel on Shorne Ridgeway. The leader of this circle was Joseph Houghton, who had come to the village in the late 1870s as the miller. He is noteworthy as the last miller to work the mill which had stood for so many centuries on Shorne Hill. A gale then 'blew off her sweps', and, although this had probably happened before in the mill's long history, windmills were by then becoming uneconomic and neither the landlords (the Trustees of Watts charity at Rochester) nor Mr Houghton thought it worth repairing, and the milling ceased. Mr Houghton continued as a baker in his cottage in the Street opposite the Rose and Crown.

He was a deeply religious man, and a group of fellow villagers began to meet in the back room of his shop. In 1890 came the last break-up of the ancient Ayerst family holdings, when part of the ancient manor (which Mr Ayerst had purchased from the Earl of Darnley in 1819 before he left the village for Bath), was put up for sale. Joseph Houghton bought the site, which comprised the whole frontage of the east side of the Street in the centre of the village between the old vicarage to the south and the cottages and outbuildings now known as

Cobb Cottage to the north. The land was still surrounded by the wall erected by Sir Roger Manwood in the sixteenth century, with the parish pump provided by Sir Roger in the middle of the frontage.

At the northern end of the site Mr Houghton dedicated a plot for a new chapel for his branch of the Methodist church. At the other end he built three cottages, calling them Ebenezer Cottages, with a new shop, bakehouse, dwelling-house and yard for his business immediately adjoining the cottages. The land between was occupied by a detached cottage and a walled garden. One may be permitted to wonder if it was the opening of the chapel, the opening of the St Katherine's chapel for catholic worship, or perhaps the activities of the Revd Canon Coates who brought with him a slight whiff of the High Church, which occasioned the words 'No Popery' in two foot high letters along the old red brick wall which enclosed Mr Houghton's purchase. Faint traces of the inscription could still be deciphered when the wall was pulled down in 1960.

An odd side incident to all this property dealing was that Mr Arnold, the Gravesend worthy and restorer of the St Katherine's chapel, also bought the ruined mill which he reconstructed as a lookout tower with a platform on the roof, giving probably the finest view in North Kent. He likewise purchased the Old Vicarage from the Revd Coates and made alterations there which altered its appearance somewhat and make it even more difficult to determine its original structure.

## Chapter 22
## THE TURN OF THE CENTURY

The parish magazine, with Canon Coates' occasional notes, enables us to follow something of village activities in the years covering the last decade of the nineteenth century and the early years of the twentieth.

When the Revd Tufnell Barrett left the village to take a living in Nottinghamshire Court Lodge was let to Mr and Mrs Winch, and Mrs Winch became the lady bountiful of the village. Children's treats were regularly provided by her, though in September 1893 the tea for the children was restricted to those from the infant school, the senior children being excluded as on a previous occasion the boys had behaved 'rudely and roughly'. She attempted to revive the ancient village fair, though she switched the date from the old St Peter's day, to the 1st of May. By the time she came to the village it seems the old fair had degenerated into a casual affair held at the behest of the local licensees, which bore little resemblance to the medieval fair held under the manor. The vestry, as the only local authority in the village at the time, had been to some trouble to get them stopped, but with what success is not clear. Mrs Winch's efforts were very different. The school children were paraded and went round the village carrying garlands and singing songs. The route seems to have been an extended one, beginning on the Ridgeway, thence to Thong Lane, then back through Shorne Ifield to the Street — over three miles. It was followed by tea in the school rooms — which must have been very welcome. The garlands and the teas were provided by Mrs Winch. The fair itself had the usual stalls and sideshows set out along the part of the Street between the churchyard entrance and Swillers Lane. Whilst the fair was on, traffic, such as it was, through the Street was more or less at a stand.

Other local activities, apart from choir and bellringers' outings and suppers, were concerts. Programmes of the concerts are usually fully set out in the Magazine, and much local talent in song and musical performances seems to have given simple pleasure several times each year to both audience and performers. One particular performance remembered by old villagers even today was the exhibition of swordsmanship given by Mr J.H. Pye of Green Farm, a member of the West Kent Yeomanry, who had won prizes for his skill. The demonstration would include the severing of a sheep carcase in two with one stroke of a heavy cavalry sword, and other movements showing skill not only with the heavy sword, but also the light sword — such items as the skilful cutting of floating silk scarves and the like.

One occasion in the village year was the parade of the Foresters' Friendly Society. The Society had a strong connection in the village, and the parade began with a procession round the village to the music of the Higham Brass Band.

In this they were often joined by other friendly societies. Some of these, like the Comical Fellows — a Society mentioned in Gravesend records in the 1820s and whose regalia was recently found in a cupboard at the Falstaff Inn on Gads Hill — have now completely disappeared. After the parade through the village the day ended with sports on the cricket meadow near Overblow, and a dinner, usually at Mr Welch's coachhouse. The Revd Coates was a member of the Society, usually taking the chair at the dinners.

One small activity of which traces occasionally occur in the parish magazine is the Shorne Club and Reading Room. It seems that a room at the old Vicarage was used for this, though it is hard to find a room there large enough for anything but a very small gathering. Concerts were often held to raise funds for the rent of the room, and a hoped-for village hall.

The 1890s witnessed an important change in secular government in the village. By this time the vestry, like the manor, had faded into insignificance. The re-organisation of urban local government in the early nineteenth century had left the rural areas untouched, whilst the introduction of the new poor law with its Unions and Guardians had removed from the parish overseers and vestry not only the administration of the poor law, but also the poor rate, which had served for so long as a source of funds for minor local administration not covered by the church rate. When the church rate was abandoned in 1871 the vestry, whatever its powers, could do little, from lack of funds.

The Local Government Act of 1894 set up Parish Councils which began an entirely new type of parochial government. It is to be regretted that the first minute book of the Shorne Parish Council appears to be lost, but the Revd Coates, who seems to have been a strong supporter of the idea of Parish Councils, frequently mentions the Council's activities in the parish magazine.

At the preliminary meeting, when members of the Council were elected, the Revd Coates was elected to the chair, and out of twenty-three nominations seven councillors were elected, and these seven promptly elected Mr Hartridge, one of the churchwardens, to be chairman of the new Council. Thus a link with the older vestry was preserved.

Under the Act the Council's powers were relatively small, but one of them was to transfer the administration of the parish charities to the Parish Council, the vicar being retained as a sort of figure head. The way in which the charities had been administered up to this time by the vicar, churchwardens, and vestry has already formed part of this story. The real difficulty was the strong dissenting connection in the village (and elsewhere of course) which objected to the church having the sole control of these charities. According to some old villagers this may well have been made worse in the village by the inability of the Methodist baker to secure the contract for the supply of bread for one of the charities which distributed bread, the contract always going outside the village to a Church of England baker. In any case a true Liberal considered that allowing unrepresentative people like vicars and churchwardens to make the distributions of the charities was totally undesirable in a democratic age. Suggestions that the money was allotted by favour would vanish if it was distributed by a democratically elected Parish Council, who would see that the money when received would not be spent on sinful pleasure.

The new Council appointed Mr Hartridge, the churchwarden, as one trustee of the new administration of the charities, but Mr A.K. Houghton, the Methodist, was the other Trustee appointed and he seems to have taken charge of the actual distribution. At the next Council meeting he reported that the list of recipients had been thoroughly revised and a book provided to record the distributions. After a year or so the distribution was further regularised by the issue of tickets to the poor which they could presumably cash with local tradesmen, but not licensees. The St Peter's Day service and sermon, followed by the distribution of cash at the church door, was discontinued.

By 1912 the parish was in receipt of quite considerable charity moneys, and it was decided that the charities must be further reorganised. To the older charities of Richard Cheney and Henry Adams, further endowments by Elizabeth Gordon, the widow of the Mr Gordon who had helped Mr Parfect in his rehabilitation of the Lady Page Charity, and Sarah Bevan, the heiress of George Startup the tanner, had been added in the late eighteenth century, whilst the expansion of the 'Poor Fund' established under the will of Sir Thomas Smythe had made an amount of about £25 a year available to the poor of the village. The righteous considered it unwise for all this money to be distributed in cash.

So Shorne United Charities was formed with the approval of the Charity Commissioners. Under the scheme then drawn up the income was to be applied in making payments to infirmaries or provident societies, the expenses of travelling to institutions, the provision of changes of air, the supply of clothes, linen etc to an amount not exceeding £5 and temporary relief by way of loan or otherwise in case of unexpected loss or sudden destitution, not exceeding £5 in any one year. All this was to be done 'in such a way as the Trustees consider most advantageous to the recipients and most conducive to the formation of provident habits'. Thus a truly democratic reorganisation of the charities at least prevented anyone from enjoying charity. With the fall in the value of money these charities have become a negligible part of parish affairs.

A more mundane matter for the Parish Council to consider was the village water supply. The dip wells on the Ridgeway were analysed, with what result is not recorded, but the real trouble was the pump in the Street. At the turn of the century the water supply began to fall, not only to the village pump, but also to Pipes Place which had a branch line from the supply provided by the springs on the hill near Overblow. Mr Arnold, as the owner of Pipes Place, at once instructed a plumber to trace the trouble, and he found the pipes from the well house in the grounds of Overblow were blocked. By this time Sir Fitzroy Maclean was the owner of Overblow, and when he found men trying to clear up the trouble on his fields, there was an explosion of exasperated protests well illustrated in the collection of lawyers' letters which have survived. He claimed the mere inspection of the water tower was a trespass, and seems to have suggested that even though the village had been receiving the water from this source for some three hundred years it had no right to water from his land. Mr Scriven, Lord Darnley's agent, was by this time chairman of the Parish Council, and he did his best to placate the angry landowner, but while the legal battle raged, the plumber got to the site and the pipes and the water tower were quietly repaired.

Happily it was not long after this that the Higham and Hundred of Hoo Water Company began the supply of piped water to the village, and the older system and the village pump fell into disuse. The pump was later removed, but the cistern into which the water once flowed is still in the garden of the cottage, and one market gardener in the village, who had a pipe fed from the old system, kept the supply to his holding going until the end of the 1939 war.

The outbreak of the Boer War caused some stir in the parish. Mr Coates in his magazine gives details of the service of various men from the village. Some six are mentioned as being in the forces, and one or two more on the reserve were called up. The vicar only reports the activities of two in any detail, and one of those has left a trail of stained glass and other changes in the church.

Rusland Tufnell Barrett, the son of the Revd Tufnell Samuel Barrett, remained in Shorne after his father had gone to Nottinghamshire, and after Court Lodge was let, resided at Woodlands Cottage on the Ridgeway, living the life of a country gentleman, hunting, steeple chasing, and horse training. It is possible the field known as Racefield between Woodlands Lane and Tanyard Hill is a relic of his activities.

He was the vicar's warden when the war broke out and at once volunteered, sailing for South Africa, there being commissioned in Thorneycroft Light Horse. One suspects influence here since when the Winches left Court Lodge, Sir Walter Hely Hutchinson, Governor of Natal, became tenant. The other local man of whom some information survives was Nigel Cook who seems to have gone out with the regular army and was under General Gatacre's command. The difference in their experiences is sufficiently marked to justify recording.

Nigel Cook seems to have spent much time in trenches repelling Boer attacks, and was finally sent home after enteric fever. Captain Barrett's career was very different. His letters to the vicar are boyish in their enthusiasm, although he was then aged about forty. In action at Val Krantz he talks of the 'Wonderful sight, shells and bullets everywhere, three hundred killed and wounded. Even better than a good run with the hounds.' A little later he received a medal for rescuing a man of his regiment under heavy fire. Then inevitably he was killed in action.

With this the Boer war fades from the parish magazine, but the church received a flurry of memorials. His hunting friends at once dedicated one stained glass window in the south aisle to his memory, while the parish collected for, and dedicated, another, both unfortunate specimens of Edwardian glass.

The collection for the parish memorial was so generously supported that there were funds left over after the window had been installed. Canon Coates then put forward what seems to have been one of his ambitions – the re-erection of the old Rood Screen in the chancel arch. When the old pews and pulpit were removed at the restoration, the remains of the screen had been removed, and stored in the vestry. Under Canon Coates' urging the remaining funds for the memorial were expended in re-erecting such of the screen as was fit, with suitable new work where the old pieces were defective, but the funds did not run to a complete restoration. Some attempt was made to collect further funds, but money was slow coming in until Mr Lacey Solomon died, and his family undertook the completion of the screen in his memory. The screen we have now is the result of this jumble of events, and though some have questioned its suitability, it is a good example of its kind, and is believed to resemble the original screen.

There seems to have been a fashion for stained glass windows in the church at about this time. Before the coming of Canon Coates the only stained glass window was the western one of the south aisle which commemorates one Jane Ball who died in 1884. At that time it seems that the rest of the windows were plain glass, making the church much lighter. The Rusland Barrett windows were quickly followed by one in memory of the Revd Marsham, and in 1907 the large east window in memory of G.W. Rhodes was inserted. Others followed, and the window in the north aisle in memory of Adelaide Hallward is of interest. During the first decade of the century Mr Hallward, a specialist in stained glass, lived in the village at Woodlands, and carried on his craft there, leaving lumps of coloured glass which are occasionally dug up around the Woodlands site. The window was a memorial to his wife 'from drawing by her'. The window, unlike all the others in the church, is Pre-Raphaelite in style, and local tradition is that the angel in the window is a portrait of one of the village girls.

In 1904 came another event in village affairs which has left a memorial in the form of the (now much altered) village hall. The efforts to raise funds for a village hall have already been mentioned, but they seem to have had little success. At the beginning of the twentieth century industry came to the village. Mention has already been made of the erection of the Uralite Works on the archeologically rich area around Stonewick Bridge on the Canal. The works may have obliterated much of archeological interest, but they also blocked the ancient way between Shorne and Higham. The Strood Rural Council took action against the company and recovered £1,000 damages. The parish at once remembered its need, and the Council released £500 towards the erection of a village hall. Mr Arnold gave a piece of land in the Street opposite the site of the old village pump, and the predecessor of our present hall was erected. The lists of concerts, meetings and general activities mentioned in the parish magazine at this time illustrate the need for a parish hall.

The parish Council was at this time accepting another change of affairs which illustrates the manner in which the semi-feudal ideas of the past were slowly dying, and marks yet another step in the long-drawn-out decline in everything manorial. The ancient common lands of the manor were by the end of the nineteenth century practically the last relic of the old manor. By this time the undefined wastes and open spaces had been generally tidied up by the encroachments we have mentioned in an earlier chapter, but the common on Shorne Hill, though by then completely dug out for gravel, was still common land, whilst the common on the Ridgeway, less well defined than the Shorne Hill area, had been dug for gravel leaving a large pit between the Ridgeway and Woodlands Lane.

The villagers by this time had little occasion to seek scrub wood for their fires, and the exact areas and rights involved were uncertain. Lord Darnley naturally wanted this tidied up. Mr Scriven, his agent, was chairman of the Parish Council, and a scheme was brought before the Council which they accepted, without much negotiation or thought. Lord Darnley carefully defined the area on Shorne Hill, and a much smaller area of land on Shorne Ridgeway (which did not include the gravel pit and its surrounding land still known as Shorne Common Rough) which he then graciously gave to the Parish as sports and recreation areas, with the clear inference that none of the adjoining land was in any way subject to common rights. Thus was an ancient link with the old manor severed.

So, one by one, several of the main themes of this history fade. The manor, the vestry, the poor, the parish charities, no longer form any intimate part of village life. Even the church's overall influence in the parish had become frayed by dissent, Roman Catholicism, and the decay of belief. Yet in 1914 the changes of the future were hardly visible. True the Mother's Union had already sampled the shape of things to come in motor char-à-banc outings to Dover and Eastbourne, and the Maidstone and District Bus Company had begun a service between Gravesend and Rochester which stopped at the Crown Half Way House as the stage coaches had done a century before. But even with a Parish Hall, a Parish Council, and a piped water supply, much of the older village life remained. Shorne was a community with few outsiders, most of its inhabitants still deeply concerned with the work of the fields around them.

## Chapter 23
## THE CHANGING VILLAGE

In retrospect, the 1914/18 war made little mark on Shorne. Army units were stationed in temporary camps around the parish, and it is said that it was the conduct of some of these troops which caused the licence of the ancient Crown Halfway House to be withdrawn, and the inn closed after so many centuries. Most of the men of service age in the village went to the war, and twenty-one names of those who lost their lives are commemorated on the war memorial in the churchyard, but the others returned to take up their old village life as it had been before the war.

At first it almost seemed as if times would not change. The Darnley interest was, if anything, increased by the erection in the early 1920s of a dower house on the ancient Puckle Hill on Shorne Ridgeway, where Lord and Lady Darnley occasionally resided whilst the Hall was let to rich Americans. Court Lodge was purchased by Major Noakes from the last of the Tufnell Barrett family, and as a descendant of the Noakes who had leased the Lodge and farm from the Gordons in the late eighteenth century, with a connection with the old Maplesden family also, one might almost imagine a return to the old small local squirearchy by one of its ancient families. But all this changed rapidly during the 1920s.

Between 1921 and 1924 government schemes to provide work began to make their mark on the roads in the parish. In 1922/3 the old Dover Road between Gravesend and Rochester was widened into a four lane highway. It followed the line of the older road along which so much history, pageantry, and poverty, had passed. At the same time the modern A2 highway between Dartford and Rochester was begun. This followed the general line of the old Roman Road which had for so long formed the southern boundary of Shorne Parish. The A2 was opened in November 1924, and, since it was an entirely new road the opening was a ceremonious affair by the Prince of Wales, with junketings at various points on the road, including a ribbon-cutting near the old Brewers Gate into Cobham Park, followed by a lunch at Cobham Hall.

With the development of the internal combustion engine, the construction of these two roads was to have a great effect on the village. Better means of communication between the village and the towns enabled many townsfolk to come to live in the country. On the other hand the wide bands of tarmacadam with the increasing traffic made Dover Road a barrier between Shorne Street and Lower Shorne, whilst the A2 constituted a similar barrier between Shorne and Cobham.

Whilst these roads were being constructed, another change was taking place in the land ownership and land use in parts of the parish. In the early 1920s the government, keen to provide 'homes fit for heroes to live in' with a nostalgic

Dairy Cottage, Shorne Ridgeway. This was one of a number of 'picturesque' cottages built around the village during the romantic revival of the early 19th century. It has been demolished and the site built over.

picture of a country of smallholders with 'three acres and a cow' began a policy of creating smallholdings. With this object in view the London County Council bought from Lord Darnley Cheneys Farm at Thong, Ifield Court Farm at Shorne Ifield, and other lands in the neighbouring parish of Chalk. These large farms were split into a number of small holdings, each with its distinctive cottage and standard barn. By 1925 the scheme was falling into disarray, and was handed over to the Kent County Council to administer. The County at once sold back into private ownership the remaining undeveloped area of Cheneys Farm, and halted the extension of the scheme. Many of the smallholders who originally took the holdings were without experience in agricultural matters and by the 1930s many of the holdings were either untenanted, or had been taken over by neighbouring farmers.

The sale of Cheneys Farm and Ifield Court farm was the beginning of the break-up of the Darnley interests in Shorne. In 1925 Lord Darnley submitted to auction a large area of his outlying estates in the district, including some four or five hundred acres of his remaining arable land in Shorne, with part of his woodlands in the parish. Some lots, mainly the woodland, did not sell, but from that time the Darnley influence in the village declined.

One of the lots offered at the sale was land on Shorne Ridgeway which is described in the particulars as a 'beautiful site for a residence of good character', and during the years which followed the building of large houses on the Ridgeway continued. Other small landowners also began the development of building plots in the Lambs Wood area on Gads Hill on the Higham boundary, and on the Lower Shorne Road. With the improvement of the Dover Road and the public transport on it, a small scatter of bungalows began to appear on these two sites, whilst some plots were sold to people who simply liked to potter about a piece of land in the country during their weekends.

Whilst this private development was going on, the Strood Rural District Council built a number of small bungalows on the Ridgeway opposite the See Ho Public House, and several houses on the Lower Shorne Road, introducing quite another class of development in the older village.

So, as time passed, parts of the village became residential areas for people from the towns. The total number of houses built was relatively small, the development being conducted at a leisurely pace and, large or small, the houses were individual units. The newcomers, being few, were easily assimilated into village life. For instance Mr Trimnell, who built a pleasant Sussex-style tiled house on the Ridgeway in 1927, became churchwarden in 1932.

Part of the estate purchased by Major Noakes was a group of old cottages near Court Lodge which, having been in the ownership of absentee landlords for many years, were in a poor condition, and the Strood Rural District Council wanted something done about them. As a result the old building which had once been the old poor house and several cottages nearby were pulled down and the awkward corner in the Street round the old poor house was made into a two-lane road, but with the yew tree which formerly stood in the garden of the old poor house still standing in the middle of the road. It is said this was at the express desire of Mrs Noakes.

In 1936 the church had another of its many restorations. The roof was found to be riddled with Death Watch beetle, the tiles were stripped off and much timber renewed. Fortunately the main king posts in the nave roof structure were sound, but the whole of the north aisle had to be re-timbered, and the restoration is recorded by the date '1936' in the plaster on the wall of the north aisle.

Changes took place in the more outlying parts of the parish. Lord Darnley, to take advantage of the growing traffic on the A2, built a restaurant by the lakes near Thong Lane, which, formerly a feature of the Cobham Hall landscaping, were cut off from the hall park by the A2. As a result of a competition the pleasant timber-built establishment was named 'Laughing Water'. Then in the late 1930s he leased the Shorne Wood nearby to the Associated Portland Cement Company for the extraction of the large bed of London clay which lay beneath the woodland. Thus the high woodland which had for so long been a feature of the village topography, renowned for its view, was excavated, the woodland destroyed, and the present abandoned wilderness created.

Another development also began in the 1930s at Thong, which though mainly outside the parish boundaries included a fringe of some twenty to thirty acres within the parish. Some enterprising speculators acquired the level farmlands on the west side of Thong Lane, and established an aerodrome, which they ambitiously named London East Airport. The whole affair, hangars and ancillary buildings, was plainly visible from Shorne Hill, the first break in the wide vista of fields and trees extending to the fringes of Gravesend, which had for so long been a feature of the view from Shorne Hill.

The Second World War halted all the changes begun in the inter-war period. The flurry of air raid precautions, the calling-up of manpower and the development of a war economy all passed quietly. The first real impact was the establishment of a Searchlight Station on the Hill near the remains of the old mill, and the requisitioning of the Aerodrome by the R.A.F.

The aerodrome was soon enlarged by extending the runways across Thong Lane towards the village, and the surrounding fields were soon dotted with the usual paraphanalia of military occupation, from barbed wire and defence posts to landing lights and telephone poles. Cobham Hall and some of the park lands, including the woods on either side of the A2, were also taken over by the R.A.F. as headquarters and for the construction of huts, air raid shelters, and other facilities for the ground staff. Traces of hut foundations, air raid shelters, and miscellaneous structures of all kinds can still be found in the woods around the A2.

If only to explain other foundations, weapon pits and matters of that sort which can still be found under the leaf mould in the woods at the junction of the Ridgeway and Woodlands Lane, it should be recorded that a transit camp was also established in that area planned to take advantage of the woodland cover, but these buildings were in fact only occupied for short periods during the build-up for the invasion of France in 1944.

The aerodrome was a fighter base, and its presence was probably the reason for the scattering of bombs of all sorts around the fields and woodlands of the parish. A relic of this still remains on the east side of the Ridgeway between Woodlands Lane and Brewers Gate, where a bomb crater is now a wayside road drainage pond. Little damage was done to property, though old oast houses at Cheneys Farm were demolished. Most of the bomb craters, like one in the middle of Mill Hill Lane near the old windmill (which may have been aimed at the searchlight station) were quickly filled in and forgotten.

Briefer, but troublesome whilst it lasted was the period of the flying bombs, when part of Shorne Ridgeway and the area of Cobham Park was included in the balloon barrage. There were several balloon sites scattered around the Ridgeway and Cobham, and from the point of view of those living near the barrage, its presence was the most dangerous period of the war. Several bombs were caught and exploded in the district, including one which fell near Woodlands Lane, hitting an army hut and killing two of the soldiers stationed there.

The formation of the Home Guard became another war factor in village affairs. As originally formed it was to be an anti-parachute watch, and for a long time it maintained a patrol on Crown Lane with its wide views across the whole river estuary, but it had two other military duties thrust upon it. During the invasion scare of August 1940 Shorne Platoon (which numbered some thirty men at the time) armed with eighteen .303 rifles and two Browning automatic rifles was ordered to man a road block which the army had constructed across the A2 near the Laughing Water Restaurant. This was one of a scattered series of defence points along an arc between the deep cutting of the London and Dover Railway at Cobham to pill boxes and an anti-tank ditch across the neck of the Hoo Peninsula between Higham and Cliffe.

Then a few months later a new defence policy was adopted. The aerodrome was the most important military installation in the district, and the crest of Shorne Hill, which as we have already remarked overlooked the aerodrome, was an important point in its defence. Accordingly Shorne Platoon was ordered to make the hill a defended locality. To help them they had, on paper, the searchlight company, a company from whatever battalion happened to be stationed at Gravesend Barracks, and an artillery battery. It was all very beautiful on paper, but the searchlight company was moved a few months later to Cobham Park, and the company from the barracks was never even contacted, but a battery of three .75s of the last war did arrive as an exercise, settled where they could be sited in an emergency, and then drove away again. The platoon dug one or two weapon pits, but the only memorial of this episode is a spigot mortar emplacement on the common with its stainless steel spigot as bright today as it was when it was installed, and which still forms an occasional subject of enquiry from passers-by.

After the war came a complete change in village life. It has two aspects. One, the very large expansion of house building and population in the parish, the other, a change in the character of the villagers.

The house building began very soon after the war, when the Strood Rural District Council acquired the old Pound Field in the village centre with a frontage to the Street and Swillers Lane, and proceeded to erect a number of Council houses of all descriptions. This involved pulling down two old buildings. One was Pound Cottage (usually known in the village as Miss Bird's cottage after a former schoolmistress who had lived there) which was one of the 'picturesque' cottages built by the Tufnell Barretts a hundred years before. The other was a curious building, a slaughter-house which stood in Swillers Lane. This had been built by Mr G.M. Arnold in one of his antiquarian forays into the village, with the remains of the old village slaughter-house which had stood in the field behind the church. The circumstances were all set out on a memorial stone on the wall of the building, which was unfortunately lost when the building was pulled down. The old village pound which stood beside Pound Cottage was also incorporated into the site. It was then only a small fenced enclosure long unused, indeed according to old villagers its only use in living memory had been for the storage of the village fire engine which had once been a piece of parish apparatus.

The Council also acquired a market garden known as Racefield on Shorne Ridgeway between the upper end of Tanyard Hill and Woodlands Lane. There were some objections to this step, but the local people were assured that it would only be used for six to eight houses. As a result we have a dozen houses on the Tanyard Hill frontage, Racefield Close with a number of old people's small bungalows, and several more council houses.

Probably the spur to the Council's building activities was the urgent need to rehouse the considerable number of squatters who had taken possession of the huts on the A2 formerly housing the R.A.F.

During the next few years estate development began in the village. Court Lodge and the field opposite, where two hundred years before the villagers had played cricket, came on the market. The house by this time had become a liability to its owners. Probably it had never been very well constructed when the Tuffnell Barretts had carried out their rebuilding a hundred years before, and by this time, in spite of the elaborate carved oak panelling and staircase, could only have been restored at great expense. The two lots were sold with planning permission for building, the house was pulled down, and the whole area covered with large detached houses by one builder, the houses having little individuality.

Shortly after this other estates were developed: Crown Green on the fields opposite Pipes Place, Cobb Drive in an orchard to the south of Pipes Place, and Manor Close on the fields around the village hall, with a scatter of a dozen or so houses on the nursery garden site on Racefield Close built privately on surplus land which had been acquired by the Strood Council and then sold off.

A more distant development must also be mentioned. After the war the aerodrome was abandoned by the R.A.F. and the requisitioned farm land on the east of Thong Lane reverted to agriculture. There was a shortlived idea of re-opening the London East Airport, but it was no longer suitable for the larger and faster modern air liner. Finally it was closed and permission given for the site to be developed for housing. The expansion of Gravesend was by this time lapping around the western boundary of the aerodrome, and between 1960 and 1970 some fifteen hundred or so houses and shops were built on the site. Of these a couple of hundred were within the old parochial boundaries of Shorne, and thus technically part of the parish. These houses are of course remote from the village, being half a mile from the cottages at Thong and well over a mile, as the crow flies, from Shorne Street. The whole block of houses of the River View Estate (as it is now called) is held back by a planning line along Thong Lane, but from the crest of Shorne Hill it shows as a menacing mass of urban development, threatening to advance and overwhelm the fields which still separate the village from the town.

Besides these main areas of building, old cottages were pulled down, and every possible corner of land in the village for which planning permission could be obtained was used for yet more new houses. The particular developments already mentioned, however, made the most conspicuous change in the appearance of the village. They created solid blocks of more or less similar houses all built at the same time, on the smallest possible areas of land per house, creating a minor urban area having no resemblance to the older village. In all about four hundred houses have been built in the parish since the war, and it cannot be assumed that the process has ceased.

Other changes in the village scene must be mentioned. In 1952 the village lost an ancient landmark. The old mill, after its conversion by Mr G.M. Arnold, had become disused, even as a lookout. Its platform had been removed, leaving a simple tower-like structure, within which was much of the original machinery, including its main centre post. In 1952 children playing around the abandoned structure started a fire which in a very short time completely destroyed the wooden upper part of the building and its ancient machinery, and today many of the newcomers to the village are not even aware of the location of what had once been a landmark which could be seen as far away as Gravesend.

In 1950 the then vicar, the Revd Claud Good, finding the vicarage built by the Revd Coates too large for his liking, sold it, and built a new vicarage on a smaller scale in its garden. Thus ended Canon Coates' dream of his vicarage serving his successors for centuries, as the Revd Coates had ended the pious intentions of Thomas Page some four and a half centuries before.

By the early 1970s the old school built on Shorne Hill a century before no longer complied with modern standards. So it was sold, the site being used for the erection of two houses, whilst a new school was constructed at the end of the newly developed Cob Drive.

After the 1939/45 war the question of a war memorial had been discussed at much length. Modern thought tended to a utilitarian rather than a monumental memorial, and it was decided that the memorial should consist of the addition of a committee room to the village hall. Mr Arthur Clark, the then owner of the meadow adjoining the hall, gave sufficient land, and a committee room and additional facilities were added, with a suitable memorial tablet on the wall recording the names of the three men from the village who had lost their lives in the last war. As with nearly all village memorials the difference in numbers between those lost in the first war and the second is a matter for remark. Then as the years passed the increasing population of the village built up pressure for more facilities. So in the 1970s the whole hall was rebuilt and enlarged, leaving the memorial committee room as but a small part of the whole complex.

Behind the bricks and mortar there has been an even more important change in the people and life of the village. This has two aspects — number and character. The census figures give details of the numbers involved, but the change of character is more difficult to describe.

The census figures tell their own story:—

| 1911 | 932 inhabitants |
| 1921 | 1,033 " |
| 1931 | 1,148 " |
| 1941 | 1,207 " |
| 1951 | 1,287 " |
| 1961 | 1,650 " |
| 1971 | 2,622 " |

The Thomas' Well by the side of the old Watling Street. Though the street was the southern boundary of the parish, the well on the south side of the road seems to have normally been treated as within Shorne parish. The well is mentioned in early parish records and was probably a recognised pilgrim's well on the way to Canterbury.

Thus it will be observed that in the years 1911 to 1941 the population increased by less than three hundred, a gradual increase easily absorbed. The figures for the last three decades tell a very different story. The increase of course includes the alien River View estate, but allowing for that, it can be seen that the population of the village itself has doubled in the twenty years between 1951 and 1971, whilst the increase of the last decade, more difficult to define because of the changes in district local government, is probably of the order of four or five hundred.

There has been an even greater change during the last thirty years in the character of those living in Shorne. The previous chapters of this history, whatever the particular subject of the chapter, have told a story of a rural parish firmly based on agriculture and the land. Even during the years between the two wars, which cannot be said to have been years of agricultural prosperity, each of the large farms in the parish, Green, Queens, Kings, and Cheneys employed eight to ten men, whilst the smaller farmers, though doing much of the work themselves, usually had at least one regular employee. Harvest was the time when additional casual labour was recruited, not only from the village itself, but from nearby parts of Gravesend. Pea picking, hop picking, and the corn harvest — the corn stooks carefully stacked by hand — were all times when casual labour supplemented the regular work force.

Thus the local farmers and those working for them, with their families, formed the principal block in the village population, whilst the non-agricultural villagers, tradesmen and town workers were fully conscious of the work on the fields around them. The farming year from seedtime to harvest was the background of the whole village life. The regular farm worker also practised crafts which had been part of the scene for centuries. For instance, even during the last war, hay and corn stacks were still the symbol of harvest, each stack being carefully thatched. I remember one of the Queens farm men, who would give the stack a thoroughly professional thatch with a fancy knob at the peak of each stack marking the completion of the harvest. No doubt he was in direct line in this handicraft with 'William a thatcher' who was buried in the churchyard in 1543 four hundred years before. The crops were carted by horses which were the carter's day-long care. Now hay and corn stacks are things of the past.

Today the same farms are worked by tractors and machines with but two or three men. The men are often skilled mechanics, though they still call the stubbles 'grattons' using the old Kentish dialect name for harvested fields, but they no longer form a perceptible proportion of the village population. The village public houses are no longer dependent on their thirsts for their trade. Indeed, the car-borne visitors from the neighbouring towns crowd the villager out of his old traditional centre of village life. When the church holds a 'Plough Sunday', apart from the impossibility of getting a three-furrow reversible plough into the church, it is also hard to find among the congregation anyone who has any connection with the fields.

To this change in the agricultural background is added another change quite different, but equally important. Before the war the children of the village went to the parish school, with its local school teachers, and on leaving the school settled into the village life of which they, even as school children, had already formed a part. Today the junior school still teaches the younger village children, though its teachers no longer expect to live in the village. Later, under the modern educational system, the children are sent to schools far from their homes for most of the day and for the remainder of their school lives. On leaving school those who do not go to university find their work in the neighbouring towns, or London, marry and settle elsewhere.

These changes have already had notable results. Take one illustration. Earlier in this history it has been mentioned that six of the Home Guards of 1940 bore the names of six of the militia of the village in Napoleonic times. The Home Guard could trace his descent from the Napoleonic militiaman. Today, only forty years later, if a new Home Guard were mustered it would not include any descendants of the Napoleonic militiamen, nor indeed of the Home Guard only a generation ago.

Another example vividly portrays the changed village life. Until the prohibition of bell ringing during the last war, the old church sexton tolled the 'passing bell' when a villager died: three strokes thrice repeated for a man and two for a woman, followed by tolling the age of the departed. Villagers in the quiet of the country-side would listen, and spare a thought for the passing of a member of the community of which they formed part. Today, if this ancient custom were revived, few would hear the bell behind the noise of passing traffic, whilst fewer still would be able to identify, or even expect to know, for whom it tolled.

To this changing village has come a flood of immigrants from the towns to occupy the hundreds of new houses. The newcomers are of all kinds. An early group were executives from the then newly established Oil Refinery on the Isle of Grain. The result of closing the refinery has yet to be seen. Several pilots from the pilotage stations of Gravesend and the Medway have settled in the village. Professional people from the neighbouring towns, managers and executives from works many miles away, retired people from the towns, all introduce a new type of population to village life.

It is perhaps too early to say what will be the final effect of these great changes. Many of the newcomers look on the village as a pleasant place in which to sleep and spend weekends, but have their principal interests elsewhere. They enjoy the fields and woods as places to walk their dogs, but the wider intimate knowledge of the fields, the farms, the crops, the seedtime and the harvest is no part of their lives.

Yet the fields, woods, and hills remain, and among the newcomers are some who learn to love the village. They take an interest in its past, take part in its current affairs, and accept the opportunities and facilities it offers. Their participation is to be wholly welcomed, because village life today is so different from the old life that the older villagers would be unable to cope with it without the co-operation of the newcomers. The active newcomer may never make the deep roots of the older, now vanishing, community, but, in the fluid world of today, neither will the descendants of the old villagers, and so as the two streams merge into a modern community, those who have adopted the village as their home help the older village to adapt itself to meet the changes of modern times. Thus under the influence of the country scenes which have formed the background of this history, we may hope that the present generation of villagers, old and new, will continue the community life of Shorne, of which this history gives some inadequate picture.

# INDEX

Adams, Henry, Charity – 46
Aerodrome at Thong – 148
Anabaptist sect in village – 130
Anglo Saxon Finds – 13
Apprenticeship of poor – 81
  Clothing of apprentice – 82
Armstrong, Edward, William, and Edward parish officers – 51
Arnold, G.M., Restores St Katherines – 137
Ayerst, Revd Thomas (Vicar) – 61
  Revd William – 79
  Revd Robert Gunsley School legacy – 124

Balam, Revd Richard (Vicar)
  his suspension – 51
Barnes, John, Minister – 58
Barrett, Capt Samuel – 112
  Carbonel Tufnell – 127
  Revd Samuel Tufnell – 133
Bastardy, its prevalence during Napoleonic Wars time – 108
Baynard, John (Yeoman) – 77
  descendant John Barnard Gentleman – 77
Bells, legacies for – 37
Bermondsey, Priory of, granted church and tithes of Shorne Parish – 17
Bethencourt, lost manor of – 14
Bickley, formerly Bichelie, a Domesday Book manor – 14
Bocton Blean Highway, old name for the Dover Road – 44
Boer War – 142
Bronze Age barrows – 9

Choir, formation of – 92
Church, description of general construction – 17, 18
  19th century restoration – 134
Churchyard, hogs in it and vicar does not consider it to be a proper place for a dunghill – 90
Churchwardens duties – 43
Charities
  See Adams, Henry
  Richard Cheney legacy – 47
  Lady Pages Apprenticeship charity, its foundation
  Its troubles – 95
  Shorne United charities – 141

Cheneys Farm – 112
Cherry harvest – 86
Cobham, Roman villa – 9
  Henry de Cobham, Lord of Randall – 25
Communion table – 51
Commons – 118 and 120
Corpus Christi, Guild of in village – 27
Court Lodge, as residence of Lords of Manor, its alteration – 127
Coates, the Revd Canon Coates (Vicar) – 136
Cricket Match between Shorne Botting family and Cobham's Baker family – 135
'Cutter' Bennett, member of Test team to Australia – 136

Davis, Goode, Life of a pauper – 84
Deadman's Bottom – 25
De Nevill, Jolan and John, Lords of Manor – 19
De Northwood, Roger, Lord of Manor – 20
Devocon money, gifts to poor – 45
Dissent in village – 129-130

Fairs, medieval – 21
  Modern – 139
Flogging of offenders – 109
Font carvings – 38
Foxe, Wigan, pauper cripple – 48
Fullers Farm – 114

Gads Hill, robberies on – 69
  Death at foot of hill – 68
Geology of district – 7
Glebe lands – 88
Gordon (Lords of Manor), Thomas – 75
  William, Elizabeth – 113
  Gift of chairs by William – 134
Gravel digging on Common – 113
Green Lane – 119

Haisden Martha marries George Woodyear, Lord of Manor – 74
Hallward, stained glass window maker in village – 143
Hawkes, Reginald – 34
Higham Ferry and causeway – 34
Home Guard – 148
Houghton, Joseph, miller and founder of primitive methodist chapel – 137

Irish refugees on Dover Road – 53

Little Moor (Tanyard) – 71

Manor of Shorne, Lords of
  De Nevill – 19
  De Northwood – 20
  Arnold Savage – 30
  George Woodyear – 73
  Thomas Gordon – 75
  Feudal services – 30
  Tenants of in 15th century – 30
Manwood, Sir Roger, presentation of village pump – 73
Maplesden,
  Jarvis I – 52
  Jarvis II – 56
  Jarvis III – 77
  Jarvis IV – 78
  Jarvis V – 79
  Jarvis VI – 80
  Jarvis V's notebook and list of inheritances – 79
Marsham, Revd Jacob (Vicar) – 133
Merston, lost village of – 13
  church of – 14
Merscfleot – 13
Methodism
  Chapel on Ridgeway – 101
  Chapel in Shorne Street – 137
Mesolithic Flints – 8
Mill, medieval –
  Hit by lightning – 111
  Last of mill – 137
Militia – 106-7

Overseers, appointment of – 42
  Duties – 42
Overblow House – 133

Page, Thomas
  Gift of vicarage to church – 35
  Other gifts
  Lady Page charity – 64
Parish Council, foundation of – 140
Parfect, Revd Caleb (Vicar) – 87
  his description of vicarage – 87
  his views on tithes – 87
  his views on bell ringing – 91
  his founding of choir – 92
Pepyr, the Revd William (Vicar) – 35
Pegion, Revd John (Vicar) – 35
Parker, Richard of Pipes Place – 55
  Henry, his son – 55
Porten, Capt, Lord of Randall Manor – 122

Railway across the parish – 131
Randall Manor, site of – 24-25
  Chapel – 25
Reed, John, licensee of the See Ho – 112
Roman remains
  Villa at Chalk – 11-12
  Villa at Cobham – 9
  Kilns – 11
  Burials – 10-12
Rood Loft and Screen – 37
  Modern Screen – 142
Rose and Crown Public House – 71
Rosse, John (Vicar) – 41
Royal Arms in church – 59

St Katherines Chapel, its possible origin – 26-27
Savage, Arnold, Lord of Manor – 30
School, Ayerst legacy – 124
  In Randall Chapel – 125
  School house on Common – 134
Shorne Mead, Common grazing – 117
  Fort – 103
Stacey, John, Minister – 58
Staines, Revd William Talbot (Vicar) – 123
Southall Thomas, Minister – 54
Solomon Joseph, Henry & Thomas, farmers – 129
Stonewick Bridge – 10
Startup, George, Tanner – 71
Sunday services – 123
Surplice worn by Revd Balam – 57

Tanyards – 71-72
Timber framed houses in village – 36-37
Tithe feast – 93
Tomlin, Thomas, Tanner – 71
  John – 96
Thames and Medway Canal – 118
Taylor, John, Lord of Manor – 75
Twopenny Attorney at law of Rochester – 96

Peninsular war, soldiers wives and families from Corunna passing through village – 107
Poor House – 101
  furniture in poor house – 102
Poor housed in Shornemead fort – 109
Public Houses
  Rose & Crown – 71
  See Ho – 69
  Crown Halfway House – 69
  Duke of York formerly Dover Castle – 69

Vicarage, Gift of old vicarage — 35
  Building of new — 136
Village Hall, its foundation  143

Water Mill — 79, 88
Water to village pump — 73
Wife buying by villager — 91
Woodyear, Lords of Manor
  George — 73
  George Junior — 74
  William — 75
  Martha — 75
Winch, Mr & Mrs at Court Lodge — 139
Work House — 109

# Meresborough Books

*Proprietors Hamish and Barbara Mackay Miller*

17 Station Road, Rainham, Gillingham, Kent. ME8 7RS
Telephone Medway (0634) 388812

We are a specialist publisher of books about Kent. Our books are available in most bookshops in the country, including our own at this address. Alternatively you may order direct, adding 10% for post (minimum 20p, orders over £20.00 post free). ISBN prefix 0 905270 for 3 figure numbers, 094819 for 4 figure numbers. Titles in print  July 1987.

**BYGONE KENT.** A monthly journal on all aspects of Kent history founded October 1979. £1.20 per month. Annual Subscription £13.00. All back numbers available.

*HARDBACKS*

**LIFE AND TIMES OF THE EAST KENT CRITIC: A Kentish Chronicle** compiled by Derrick Molock. Large format. ISBN 3077. £9.95.

**THE PAST GLORY OF MILTON CREEK: Tales of Slipways, Sails and Setting Booms** compiled by Alan Cordell and Leslie Williams. ISBN 3042. £9.95.

**TALES OF VICTORIAN HEADCORN or The Oddities of Heddington** by Penelope Rivers (Ellen M. Poole). ISBN 3050. £8.95. (Also available in paperback ISBN 3069. £3.95.)

**ROCHESTER FROM OLD PHOTOGRAPHS** compiled by the City of Rochester Society. Large format. ISBN 975. £7.95. (Also available in paperback ISBN 983. £4.95.)

**THE LONDON, CHATHAM & DOVER RAILWAY** by Adrian Gray. A major study of the development of railways in Kent. ISBN 886. £7.95.

**THE NATURAL HISTORY OF ROMNEY MARSH** by Dr F.M. Firth, M.A., Ph.D. ISBN 789. £6.95.

O FAMOUS KENT by Eric Swain. The county of Kent in old prints. ISBN 738. £9.95. BARGAIN OFFER £4.95.

KENT'S OWN by Robin J. Brooks. The history of 500 (County of Kent) Squadron of the R.A.A.F. ISBN 541. £5.95.

TWO HALVES OF A LIFE by Doctor Kary Pole. The autobiography of a Viennese doctor who escaped from the Nazis and established a new career in Kent. ISBN 509. £5.95.

SOUTH EAST BRITAIN: ETERNAL BATTLEGROUND by Gregory Blaxland. A military history. ISBN 444. £5.95.

STRATFORD HOUSE SCHOOL 1912-1987 by Susan Pittman. A well illustrated history. ISBN 3212. £10.00.

A NEW DICTIONARY OF KENT DIALECT by Alan Major. The first major work on the subject this century. ISBN 274. £7.50.

KENT CASTLES by John Guy. The first comprehensive guide to all the castles and castle sites in Kent. ISBN 150. £7.50.

US BARGEMEN by A.S. Bennett. A new book of sailing barge life around Kent and Essex from the author of 'June of Rochester' and 'Tide Time'. ISBN 207. £6.95.

THE GILLS by Tony Conway. A history of Gillingham Football Club. 96 large format pages packed with old photographs. ISBN 266. £5.95. BARGAIN OFFER £1.95.

A VIEW OF CHRIST'S COLLEGE, BLACKHEATH by A.E.O. Crombie, B.A. ISBN 223. £6.95.

JUST OFF THE SWALE by Don Sattin. The story of the barge-building village of Conyer. ISBN 045. £5.95.

TEYNHAM MANOR AND HUNDRED (798-1935) by Elizabeth Selby, MBE. ISBN 630. £5.95.

THE PLACE NAMES OF KENT by Judith Glover. A comprehensive reference work. ISBN 614. £7.50 (also available in paperback. ISBN 622. £3.95)

*LARGE FORMAT PICTORIAL PAPERBACKS*

EAST KENT FROM THE AIR by John Guy. 50 photographs from the Cambridge University collection. ISBN 3158. £3.50.

WEST KENT FROM THE AIR by John Guy. 50 photographs from the Cambridge University collection ISBN 3166. £3.50.

ARE YOU BEING SERVED, MADAM? by Molly Proctor. A pictorial history of Drapers Shops in Kent. ISBN 3174. £3.50.

OLD BROADSTAIRS by Michael David Mirams. A collection of old photographs. ISBN 3115. £3.50.

OLD PUBS OF TUNBRIDGE WELLS & DISTRICT by Keith Hetherington and Alun Griffiths. A well researched pictorial history with 154 illustrations. ISBN 300X. £3.50.

GOUDHURST: A Pictorial History by John T. Wilson, M.A. ISBN 3026. £2.95.

A PICTORIAL STUDY OF ALKHAM PARISH by Susan Lees and Roy Humphreys. ISBN 3034. £2.95.

THE MOTOR BUS SERVICES OF KENT AND EAST SUSSEX — A brief history by Eric Baldock. An illustrated history from 1899 to 1984 containing 146 photographs. ISBN 959. £4.95.

ROCHESTER FROM OLD PHOTOGRAPHS — see under hardbacks.

PEMBURY IN THE PAST by Mary Standen. ISBN 916. £2.95.

OLD MARGATE by Michael David Mirams. ISBN 851. £3.50.

EXPLORING OLD ROCHESTER by John Bryant. A guide to buildings of historic interest. ISBN 827. £2.95.

THOMAS SIDNEY COOPER OF CANTERBURY by Brian Stewart. The life and work of Britain's best cattle painter, with 10 illustrations in colour. ISBN 762. £2.95.

KENT TOWN CRAFTS by Richard Filmer. A pictorial record of sixteen different crafts. ISBN 584. £2.95.

OLD CHATHAM: A THIRD PICTURE BOOK by Philip MacDougall. Another collection of old photographs. ISBN 3190. £3.50.

SMARDEN: A PICTORIAL HISTORY by Jenni Rodger. ISBN 592. £2.95.

A PICTUREBOOK OF OLD SHEPPEY by Michael Thomas. 130 Old photographs, mostly from glass negatives. ISBN 657. £2.95.

FIVE MEDWAY VILLAGES by Wyn Bergess and Stephen Sage. A pictorial history of Aylesford, Burham, Wouldham, Eccles and Borstal. ISBN 649. £2.95.

OLD SANDWICH by Julian Arnold and Andrew Aubertin. 146 old photographs. ISBN 673. £2.95.

AVIATION IN KENT by Robin Brooks. A pictorial history from 19th century ballooning to 1939. ISBN 681. £2.95.

THE LIFE AND ART OF ONE MAN by Dudley Pout. A Kentish farmer's son who became successful as a commercial artist and as a children's illustrator. ISBN 525. £2.95.

OLD MAIDSTONE'S PUBLIC HOUSES by Irene Hales. 123 photographs. ISBN 533. £2.95.

OLD MAIDSTONE Vol. 1 by Irene Hales and Kay Baldock. ISBN 096. £2.50.

OLD MAIDSTONE Vol. 2 by Irene Hales. ISBN 38X. £2.50.

OLD TONBRIDGE by Don Skinner. ISBN 398. £2.50.

KENT TRANSPORT IN OLD POSTCARDS by Eric Baldock. 146 photographs. ISBN 320. £2.95.

GEORGE BARGEBRICK Esq. by Richard-Hugh Perks. The story of Smeed Dean Ltd in Sittingbourne. 80 illustrations. ISBN 479. £4.50.

*STANDARD SIZE PAPERBACKS*

KENT COUNTRY CHURCHES by James Antony Syms. A reprint of his first very popular collection of drawings. ISBN 3131. £4.50.

KENT COUNTRY CHURCHES CONTINUED by James Antony Syms. A second collection of drawings. ISBN 314X. £5.95.

KENT INNS AND SIGNS by Michael David Mirams. A book for all interested in the origins of pub names and signs. ISBN 3182. £3.95.

EXPLORING SUSSEX CHURCHES by John E. Vigar. A companion to 'Exploring Kent Churches'. ISBN 3093. £3.95.

A WEALDEN VILLAGE: MARDEN by Phyllis Highwood and Peggy Skelton. A well researched book for all interested in Wealden history. ISBN 3107. £4.95.

EXPLORING KENT CHURCHES by John E. Vigar. What to look for when visiting a church. ISBN 3018. £3.95.

FLIGHT IN KENT. Another selection of articles by members of the Kent Aviation Historical Research Society. ISBN 3085. £1.95.

**TALES OF VICTORIAN HEADCORN** — see under hardbacks.

**BIRDWATCHING IN KENT** by Don Taylor. Details of when and where to watch for which birds, plus very readable accounts of personal experiences. ISBN 932. £4.50.

**CRIME AND CRIMINALS IN VICTORIAN KENT** by Adrian Gray. An insight into an intriguing if unsavoury side of Victorian life in Kent. ISBN 967. £3.95.

**CHIDDINGSTONE — AN HISTORICAL EXPLORATION** by Jill Newton. ISBN 940. £1.95.

**STOUR VALLEY WALKS** from Canterbury to Sandwich by Christopher Donaldson. Enjoy six days walking along the route taken by Caesar, Hengist & Horsa, St Augustine and many others. ISBN 991. £1.95.

**THE GHOSTS OF KENT** by Peter Underwood, President of the Ghost Club. ISBN 86X. £3.95.

**CURIOUS KENT** by John Vigar. A selection of the more unusual aspects of Kent history. ISBN 878. £1.95.

**COBHAM.** Published for Cobham Parish Council. ISBN 3123. £1.00.

**A CHRONOLOGY OF ROCHESTER** by Brenda Purle. ISBN 851. £1.50.

**SITTINGBOURNE & KEMSLEY LIGHT RAILWAY STOCKBOOK AND GUIDE.** ISBN 843. 95p.

**DOVER REMEMBERED** by Jessie Elizabeth Vine. Personal memories from the early years of this century. ISBN 819. £3.95.

**THE PLACE NAMES OF KENT** — see under hardbacks.

**PENINSULA ROUND** (The Hoo Peninsula) by Des Worsdale. ISBN 568. £1.50.

**A HISTORY OF CHATHAM GRAMMAR SCHOOL FOR GIRLS, 1907-1982** by Audrey Perkyns. ISBN 576. £1.95.

**CYCLE TOURS OF KENT** by John Guy. No. 1: Medway, Gravesend, Sittingbourne and Sheppey. ISBN 517. £1.50.

**WINGS OVER KENT.** A selection of articles by members of the Kent Aviation Historical Research Society. ISBN 69X. £1.95.

**LULLINGSTONE PARK: THE EVOLUTION OF A MEDIAEVAL DEER PARK** by Susan Pittman. ISBN 703. £3.95.

**LET'S EXPLORE THE RIVER DARENT** by Frederick Wood. Walking from Westerham to Dartford. ISBN 770. £1.95.

**SAINT ANDREW'S CHURCH, DEAL** by Gregory Holyoake. ISBN 835. 95p.

**BIRDS OF KENT:** A Review of their Status and Distribution. A reprint, with addendum, of the 448 page study by the Kent Ornithological Society. ISBN 800. £6.95.

**FROM MOTHS TO MERLINS:** The History of West Walling Airfield by Robin J. Brooks. ISBN 3239. £4.95.

**KENT AIRFIELDS IN THE BATTLE OF BRITAIN.** The story of nine airfields in Kent in 1940 told by members of the Kent Aviation Historical Research Society — a paperback reprint. ISBN 3247. £4.95.

**SHORNE:** The History of a Kentish Village by A.F. Allen. A well researched history from earliest times. ISBN 3204. £4.95.

**SHERLOCK HOLMES AND THE KENT RAILWAYS** by Kelvin Jones. A study of the master detective's forages into Kent. ISBN 3255. £8.95.